Charles Michael Baggs

The Ceremonies of the Holy-Week at Rome

Charles Michael Baggs

The Ceremonies of the Holy-Week at Rome

1st Edition | ISBN: 978-3-73409-613-6

Place of Publication: Frankfurt am Main, Germany

Year of Publication: 2019

Outlook Verlag GmbH, Germany.

THE CEREMONIES

OF THE

HOLY-WEEK

AT ROME.

BY

THE RT. REV. MONSIGNOR BAGGS,

BISHOP OF PELLA.

THIRD EDITION.

ROME:

SOLD BY LUIGI PIALE,

ENGLISH BOOKSELLER,

1. PIAZZA DI SPAGNA, 106. VIA BABUINO.

1854.

DIRECTIONS

FOR SEEING THE CEREMONIES

Provide yourself with a **Holy-Week-book**, or *Uffizio della Settimana Santa*. Take care that your dress is according to rule. For many of the ceremonies ladies require tickets signed by *M. Maggiordomo*.

On Palm-sunday morning the Pontifical ceremonies begin at S. Peter's, at about 9 o'clock: no stranger can receive a palm without a permission signed by *M. Maggiordomo*. In the afternoon the Card. Penitentiary goes at about 4 or half past 4 to S. John Lateran's, where the Station of the day is held.

On the *afternoons* of *Wednesday* and *Thursday*, (between 4 and half past 4) and of *Friday* (half an hour sooner) the office of Tenebræ begins at the Sixtine chapel. After it is over, you may go to S. Peter's to bear the conclusion of a similar service: there on Thursday evening the high-altar is washed by the Card, priest and chapter; on Friday the Pope, Cardinals etc. go thither to venerate the relics after Tenebræ in the Sixtine chapel; and on the afternoons of both days the Card. Penitentiary goes thither in slate. In the evening of these three days the feet of pilgrims are washed, and they are served at table by Cardinals etc. at the Trinità dei Pellegrini.

On *Thursday morning* you can see the oils blessed at S. Peter's: this ceremony begins *early*. There is little difference between the mass (at about half past 9 or 10) in the Sixtine chapel on this day, and on ordinary days, and there is generally a great crowd: the procession after mass is repeated on the following morning; and the papal benediction on Easter Sunday: your best plan therefore will be to go at an early hour to see the blessing of the oils, and afterwards the washing of the feet, at S. Peter's; and then go to see the dinner of the *apostles* near the balcony from which the Pope gives His benediction. The *Sepulchres*, particularly that in the Cappella Paolina, may be visited.

On *Friday morning* the service of the Sixtine chapel begins at about half past 9 or 10. (Devotion of 3 hours' agony from about half past 12 to half past 3 at the Gesù, SS. Lorenzo e Damaso etc.; after the *Ave Maria* the *Via Crucis* at Caravita, and devotion of the dolours of the B. Virgin at S. Marcello, etc. An hour after the *Ave Maria* poetical compositions are recited at the Serbatojo dell'Arcadia).

On *Saturday morning* service begins at S. John Lateran's at about half past 7. As soon you have seen the baptism at the baptistery, you had better drive to the Vatican, to attend at the beautiful mass of the Sixtine chapel.

On *Saturday afternoon* you may go to the Armenian mass at S. Biagio or S. Gregorio Illuminatore: it begins towards 4 o clock. On Easter-Sunday the Pope sings solemn mass at S. Peter's, at about 9 o'clock. He afterwards venerates the relics, and gives His solemn benediction. In the afternoon, besides Vespers there is a procession at S. Peter's called that of the 3 Maries. (At S. John Lateran's the Cardinals assist at Vespers, and afterwards venerate the relics preserved there) At night the cupola is illuminated, and on the following night there are fireworks or *girandola* at Castle S. Angelo. On Monday, Tuesday, and Saturday there is *cappella papale* at the Vatican, but it differs little from the ordinary *cappelle*.

CHAP. I.

ON THE CEREMONIES OF THE MASS

CONTENTS.

Origin of the word *ceremony*—object of ceremonies—institution of the mass—its earliest ceremonies—discipline of secrecy—liturgy of the Roman church—general review of the principal ceremonies of the mass —mass of the catechumens, *ambones*—mass of the faithful, blessed water, secrecy, prayers for the dead—Latin the language of the Roman liturgy, and why—usual ceremonies of high-mass in the papal chapel— sentiments of S. John Chrysostom.

"It was chiefly, if not only, in the mystical liturgy of the eucharist, that the primitive church spoke without reserve of all the sublimities of Christian faith." Palmer, Origines Liturg. vol. I, p. 13.

|*Origin of the word ceremony.*

From Rome our Saxon forefathers received Christianity; and from the same source we have derived several words denoting Christian rites. Thus the words *religion, sacrament, sacrifice, communion*, and others are Latin, with the exception of the termination. The word *ceremony* also is Latin, and owes its origin to an interesting fact in ancient Roman history. When the Capitol was besieged by the Gauls (A.U. 365) most of the inhabitants of Rome provided for their own safety by flight: but the Flamen Quirinalis or priest of Romulus, and the Vestal virgins loaded themselves with the sacred things, that they might secure those hallowed treasures from profanation. "They were proceeding" (says Livy lib. V, c. XXII) "along the way which passes over the Sublician bridge, when they were met on the declivity by L. Albinus a plebeian, who was fleeing with his wife and children in a *plaustrum* or cart: he and his family immediately alighted: then placing in the cart the virgins and sacred things he accompanied them to Cære where they were received with hospitality and respect". Hence (says Valerius Maximus lib. I, c. 1.) "sacred things were called ceremonies, because the inhabitants of *Cære* revered them when the republic was broken, as readily as when it flourished". Thus is the word ceremony associated at once with the devotion of Albinus, with the Gaulish invasion of the Capitol, and with Cære, one of the twelve cities of Etruria, now called Cervetri or Cære vetus[1]. The Pagan Romans derived their religious rites from Etruria, and in particular from Cære on account of its proximity to Rome: this may be another reason for the adoption of the term *ceremony*, which was afterwards applied to the rites of all religions[2].

Object of ceremonies.

But what, it may be asked by many, is the use of ceremonies? I shall answer in the words of the council of Trent. "Since the nature of man is such, that he cannot easily without exterior helps be raised to the meditation of divine things, the church as a pious mother has instituted certain rites, namely, that some things in the mass should be pronounced in a low voice and others aloud; she has also used ceremonies, as mystical benedictions, lights, incense, vestments, and many other things of that kind, from apostolical tradition and discipline, in order that the majesty of so great a sacrifice might be displayed, and the minds of the faithful might be excited by these visible signs of religion and piety to the contemplation of those sublime things which are concealed in this sacrifice". Session XXII, c. V.—These words lead us to treat briefly of the mass, the principal act of divine worship during holy-week as at all other seasons of the year. This we do now the more readily, that we may not afterwards be obliged to interrupt our account of the peculiar ceremonies of Holy week, which presuppose an acquaintance with the mass.

Institution of the mass.

Jesus Christ instituted the mass at his last supper, when he took bread and blessed and broke and gave to his disciples and said, Take ye and eat, this is my body; and taking the chalice he gave thanks, and gave to them saying, Drink ye all of this: For this is my blood of the new testament, which shall be shed for many unto remission of sins: Matth. XXVI, 26. In this brief account are mentioned all the *essential* parts of the mass. Christ commanded the apostles and through them their successors to perform the same holy rite "in commemoration" of Him, and they obeyed His commands, as we learn from the acts of the apostles, and the first epistle to the Corinthians.

Its early ceremonies.

Gradually various prayers and ceremonies were added to the sacred words pronounced by Christ, as the Apology of St. Justin, the writings of St. Cyprian, the catechetical discourses of St. Cyril of Jerusalem and other early works prove. The Apostles themselves had added the Lord's prayer[3]. The liturgy however during the first four centuries, as Le Brun maintains[4], or, according to Muratori followed by Palmer, the first three centuries, was not written, but was preserved by oral tradition, according to the received practice of the early church, which, unwilling to give what is holy to dogs, or to cast pearls before swine concealed from all persons, except the faithful, the mysteries of faith. It would seem from St. Justin's apology, that much was left to the particular devotion of the bishop or priest who offered mass, and hence we might expect not to find in the earliest liturgies great uniformity, except in essentials and general outline. Yet Le Brun has endeavoured to restore, from the early Christian writers, the liturgy used in the first four centuries: and it contains the most important prayers and ceremonies of the mass in its more modern form.

Discipline of secrecy.

We shall so often have to recur to the discipline of secrecy alluded to above, that we consider it necessary to speak of it briefly, before we proceed further. The Pythagoreans, the Stoics, Plato, the Epicureans and other ancient philosophers concealed their doctrines from the uninitiated: the mysteries also of Osiris, Isis, Bacchus, Ceres, Cybele etc. were carefully kept secret. There was no novelty therefore for the ancients in the discipline of secrecy, the institution of which in the Christian church is attributed by many fathers to Christ himself, who directed that his disciples should not "give what is holy to dogs, or cast pearls before swine". Matt. VII, 6. This injunction was observed by the whole church from the apostolic age till the fifth century in the east, and the sixth century in the west: it extended to dogmas as well as rites, and in particular to those of the holy Trinity and the sacraments, especially the blessed Eucharist[5]. For "those things" says St. Cyril of Alexandria "are generally derided, which are not understood" adv. Julianum. The pagans, at the instigation, it would appear, of the Jews and early heretics, availed themselves of this secret discipline to charge the Christians with the detestable crimes of Oedipus and Thyestes, pretending that in their secret assemblies they murdered an infant covered with flour, and drank his blood. (Cecilius ap. Minut. Fel.) It was solely with the view of refuting these calumnies, that Justin Martyr explained, in his apology addressed to Antoninus Pius, the catholic doctrine of the eucharist. S. Blandina on the contrary endured the most cruel torments rather than reveal it, though its profession would have confuted the same odious calumnies; and S. Augustine observes a similar reserve when answering the pagan Maximus Madaurensis.

"Who" says the protestant Casaubon "is so little versed in the writings of the fathers, as to be ignorant of the formulary used principally of the sacraments, the initiated understand what is said: it occurs at least fifty times in Chrysostom, and almost as frequently in Augustine". S. Fulgentius inserts in his answer to the deacon Ferrandus the following words of S. Augustine to the neophytes "This which you see on the altar of God you saw last night: but what it was, what it meant, and of what a great thing it contains the sacrament, you have not yet heard. What therefore you see is bread and the chalice. What your faith demands is, that the bread is the body of Christ, and the chalice contains the blood of Christ". S. Cyril of Jerusalem in his catechetical discourses addressed to the newly baptised inculcates in the strongest terms the doctrine of the real presence, but charges them most strictly not to communicate to the catechumens his instructions. In consequence of this practice the early fathers often speak obscurely of the B. Sacrament, and call it bread and wine and *fermentum* after the consecration, though they clearly teach the *faithful* the doctrine of the real presence[6].

|*Liturgy of the Roman church.*

Pope Innocent I, writing to Decentius at the beginning of the fifth century, attributes the liturgy of the Roman church to St. Peter. It was first written in the fifth century; and Pope Vigilius sending it in 538 to Profuturus derives it from Apostolic tradition. The most ancient sacramentary or liturgical work extant of the Roman church is that of Gelasius who was Pope from 492 to 496[7]. He collected prayers composed by more ancient authors, and also composed some himself: and this Gelasian compilation was reformed by Gregory the Great and reduced to one volume[8], which may be considered as the prototype of our present liturgy. The canon or most solemn part of the mass has been preserved inviolate ever since, as appears from the Ordines Romani written shortly after the time of S. Gregory, and also from the explanations of it written by Florus and Amalarius. This canon as well as the order of prayer are the same as those of Gelasius, as Palmer observes (Orig. liturg. vol. 1, p. 119,) and are also nearly identical with those of the sacramentary of S. Leo. The Ambrosian and African liturgies also were evidently derived at a very remote period from that of Rome. From such considerations as these Mr. Palmer proves the very ancient or apostolical origin of the "main order", the substance of the Roman liturgy. Origines liturg. vol. I, sect. VI. The author of the canon is unknown; yet we know the authors of some additions to the canon. Thus S. Leo I added sanctum sacrificium immaculatam hostiam, S. Gregory I, diesque nostros in tua pace disponas.

|*Review of the ceremonies of the mass.*

|*Mass of the catechumens, ambones, sermons.*

We shall not examine minutely all the prayers and ceremonies of the mass, or stop to enquire at what time and by what pope each of them was first introduced, lest we should weary the patience of our readers[9]; but we shall content ourselves with a general review of the mass, as it is now celebrated. We may divide it, as the ancients did, into two parts, the mass of the catechumens, and the mass of the faithful. The first part includes the preparation and confession of sins at the foot of the altar, the *introit* or anthem and part of a psalm sung at the *entrance* into church, the *Kyrie eleison* or petition for mercy, the *Gloria in excelsis* or hymn of praise (both of great antiquity, as Palmer following our catholic divines has shewn) the collect or collects so called from their being said when the people are collected together, the epistle and gospel, and also the verses, said or sung between them both, called the Gradual[10]: if sung by one voice, it is called the Tract; if by choir, the Responsory. The collects and other prayers are said with the arms extended in the same manner as many figures are represented praying on old christian as well as pagan monuments. After the gospel the sermon used to be preached, as it generally is in our times[11] and after the sermon Pagans, Jews, heretics, schismatics, energumens, public penitents and catechumens were dismissed by the deacon; for the faithful alone were allowed to be present at the celebration of the sacred mysteries, in conformity to the discipline of secrecy. That part of mass, which we have described was called the mass of the catechumens, because these were allowed to be present at it.

Mass of the faithful, blessed water.

From the *missio, missa,* or dismissal announced by the deacon to the people before and after the mass of the faithful, the term *missa* or mass is derived. It was in use in the early ages; for it is found not only in the epistle to the bishop of Vienne attributed to Pope Pius I, and in that of Pope Cornelius to Lupicinus: but S. Ambrose also says "I continued my duty, and began to celebrate mass" and in another place he exhorts the people to "hear mass daily[12]".

When the church had been cleared of all except the faithful, the second part of our mass, or the mass of the faithful, began with the Nicene symbol or creed. Then followed the offertory, or part of a psalm sung anciently while the people made their offerings to the church, particularly of bread and wine[13]. The priest offers to God the bread, and wine mixed according to apostolic tradition[14] with a little water, which our Saviour is believed to have mixed with the wine at the last supper; he implores God's blessing on these offerings, and washes his hands in token of the purity of soul[15] with which the sacred mysteries should be approached, and at high mass for the sake of outward cleanliness also, on account of the incense which he has used. Having commemorated the passion, resurrection, and ascension of Christ, as he does also after the consecration, he calls on those present to join him in prayer, he says another prayer or prayers called the *secret*, because said in secret, and then recites the *preface* to the canon, a prayer in which he unites with the celestial spirits in praise and thanksgiving as Christ himself gave thanks at the last supper: it concludes with the Tersanctus or Trisagion "Holy, Holy, Holy etc." which, as Palmer observes, has been probably used in the Christian liturgy of the east and west since the ages of the apostles. V. 2. p. 219.

The canon of the mass next follows, which as well as many of the preceding and following prayers is said in a low voice, according to the ancient custom alluded to by Innocent I, S. Augustine, Origen, and other Fathers[16]. In it the priest prays for the church, the Pope, the bishop of the place, the living and the dead[17] he reveres the memory of the B. Virgin, the Martyrs and other Saints[18], and having once more implored the blessing of God, and spread his hands over the victim, according to the custom of the Jews, he pronounces over the bread and wine the words of consecration according to the command of Christ, and adores and raises for the adoration of the people the body and blood of our Divine Lord. It is in this consecration that the sacrifice of the mass principally consists; as by it the victim is placed on the altar, and offered to God, viz. Christ himself, represented as dead by the separate consecration of the bread and wine, as if His blood were separated from His body. After some other prayers, in which the priest offers to God the holy sacrifice, and prays for mercy and salvation for all present, he elevates the host and chalice together; this was the ancient elevation, as the more solemn one, which follows immediately after the consecration, was introduced generally in the 12th century, in opposition to the heresy of Berengarius. Then concluding the canon the priest recites the *Our Father*, and breaks the host, as Christ broke the bread, and as His body was "broken" for us[19]; he puts a particle of the host into the chalice[20]; he implores mercy and peace from the lamb of God, at solemn masses gives the kiss of peace according to the recommendation of scripture, and receives the two ablutions of the chalice, one of wine, the other of wine and water, lest any portion of the sacred blood should remain in it: he recites the communion or anthem, which was originally sung while the holy communion was distributed; he says the prayer or prayers called postcommunion, dismisses and begs God's blessing on the people, in fine he recites the beginning of St. John's gospel or some other gospel appropriate to the day. We shall on other occasions recur to various ceremonies of the mass[21].

Latin the language of the liturgy.

The language of our liturgy has descended to us as a precious legacy from the time when Peter and Paul preached in Rome. It would be incongruous that our ancient hierarchy robed in ancient vestments should perform our ancient liturgy in a moderne language. As in all parts of the globe there are members of the Catholic church, she has wisely preserved in her liturgy a language common to all countries, the language too of majesty, civilisation and science, as De Maistre observes. Like her divine founder she is the same yesterday and to-day: like the rock, on which she is built, she is proof against the winds and waves; she is unchanged and unaffected by the wayward caprices of fashion. Translations of her liturgy are published for the use of those who are unacquainted with Latin so that they may either join in reciting the prayers of the church, or say others which their own devotion may suggest.

Having described the ceremonies of low-mass, we shall subjoin a brief account of those customary at high-mass when celebrated in the papal chapel: we shall thus avoid unnecessary repetitions in the course of this work. The beginning of the mass is said by all persons within the sanctuary: and the Pope recites it before the altar with the celebrant. As His Holiness is the ecclesiastical superior of the latter, and is habited in his sacred vestments, many benedictions are, according to a general rubric, reserved to Him, which are otherwise given by the person who sings mass. Thus He blesses not only the incense, the water at the offertory, the subdeacon and deacon, the preacher, when there is a sermon, and the people after the sermon and at the end of mass, but also the Cardinals on several occasions, and the celebrant himself before he offers up mass. "For without contradiction (says St. Paul) that which is less is blessed by the better". Hebr. VII, 7. He also, and not the celebrant, kisses the book of the Gospel. The first cardinal priest present hands to Him the incense, and also incenses him, kneeling down if the Pope be seated at the time, and standing if the Pope stands[22], and therefore, he is seated near the Pope during part of the Mass, that he may be ready when his services are required.

Incense is used, as is customary at high masses, before the introit, at the Gospel, after the offertory and during the elevation. Before the introit the crucifix, the altar[23], the celebrant and the Pope are successively incensed. Before the deacon sings the gospel he incenses the book; and after it the Pope is once more incensed by the first cardinal priest. After the offertory, besides the bread and wine, the crucifix, the altar, the celebrant and the Pope, the Cardinals and the first in rank among the prelates and other personages are incensed by the deacon. At the elevation the blessed Sacrament alone is incensed.[24]

When the Pope reads from the missal, this book is held by the first, and a taper by the second, patriarch or assisting bishop[25]. The *Kyrie eleison*, the *Gloria in excelsis, Credo, Sanctus* and *Agnus Dei* are said by all persons within the sanctuary: the cardinals descend from their seats to say them, and form a circle in the middle of the chapel; having received the Pope's blessing they return to their places. After the *Sanctus*, the Pope goes before the middle of the altar followed by the assistant bishops and others of His train's and all kneel till the elevation is ended. After the *Agnus Dei*, the first Card. priest goes up to the altar, kisses it, and receives from the celebrant the kiss of peace: this he gives to the Pope, from whom the two first Card. deacons receive it. The Card. priest then returns to his place, and gives the kiss of peace to the priest who assists the celebrant; from him the first of the other cardinals and principal prelates receive it and communicate it to their colleagues. The assistant priest then gives it to the master of ceremonies, who has accompanied him, from whom the other colleges of prelates receive it and in fine (if time permit) to the deacon, from whom it passes to others who assist at the altar. When the pope gives His blessing, the cross is held before Him by the last auditor of the rota, and His vestment by the first protonary. Such are the ceremonies generally observed at high mass in the papal chapel, except at masses for the dead, when some of them, and in particular those of incensing (except at the offertory and elevation) and of the kiss of peace, are omitted.

|*Sentiments of S. John Chrysostom.*

We shall conclude with the words of a holy and eloquent bishop of Costantinople of the 4th century, "When thou seest the Lord immolated and placed there, and the priest engaged in the sacrifice and praying, and all present empurpled with precious blood, dost thou think that thou art among men, and art standing on the earth? and not rather that thou art instantaneously transferred to heaven, where casting out of thy soul every fleshly thought thou lookest around on heavenly things. O miracle! O the love of God for man! He, who sits above with the Father, is at the same time held in the hands of all, and gives himself to those who wish to receive and embrace him. Wishest thou to see the excellence of this *holiness* from another miracle? Depict before thy eyes Elias and an innumerable multitude surrounding him, and the victim placed on the stones; all the others in profound silence, and the prophet alone praying; then suddenly fire rushing from heaven on the sacrifice. These things are astonishing and replete with wonder. Then transfer thyself thence to the things now effected, and thou wilt find them not only wonderful, but surpassing all astonishment. For here the priest bears not fire, but the holy Ghost; he pours out long supplications, not that fire descending from above may consume the offerings, but that grace falling on the sacrifice may through it inflame the souls of all and render them purer than silver purified by fire. This most dread rite then who, that is not altogether insane and out of his mind, shall be able to contemn? Art thou ignorant that no human soul could have sustained this fire of the victim, but all would have totally perished, unless the assistance of divine grace had been abundant" S. John Chrysostom, De Sacerdotio Lib. 3, c. IV.

Footnote 1: (return)

It is situated near the road leading from Rome to Civitavecchia at the distance of about 27 miles from the former city. Its necropolis has lately enriched the new

Gregorian museum with some of its most precious treasures, consisting in gold ornaments of the person, in silver and painted vases etc. of very ancient and admirable execution. See Nibby, Analisi storico-topografica etc. as also Grifi. The Etruscan and Egyptian museums entitle His present Holiness Gregory XVI to be ranked with many of His predecessors among the greatest and most munificent patrons and collectors of ancient monuments.

Footnote 2: (return)

If we compare with this term others of similar termination, such as *sanctimonia* from *sanctus*, we shall find in them a confirmation of the etymology given above: *monia* serves to form the substantive, but does not otherwise alter the meaning.

Footnote 3: (return)

S. Greg. M. lib. VII, epist. 64.

Footnote 4: (return)

See Le Brun, Explic. Missae T. 2. dis. 1. Also Renaudot. They have however been refuted by Assemani, Maratori and Zaccaria.

Footnote 5: (return)

The *Pater noster* is still said in secret, except after the canon of the Mass, because at that part of the Liturgy only the faithful were present. See Moroni's learned work entitled, Dizionario di erudizione ecclesiastica.

Footnote 6: (return)

See Schelstratius, de Disciplina Arcani, or Trevern's answer to Faber's Difficulties of Romanism: also Bingham lib. X, c. 5. Times are now so much altered that it is difficult to conceive how the Reserve in communicating Religious knowledge recommended in one of the Tracts for the Times could be practicable, even if it were judged expedient.

Footnote 7: (return)

It was first published by B. Card. Tommasi from a very ancient manuscript in the queen of Sweden's library. Cave, Mabillon, Muratori, Assemani and other eminent critics admit its authenticity. There is however another sacramentary *perhaps* more ancient called the Leonian, because it is attributed by the learned to Leo the great, A.D. 450. It was first published by Bianchini in the 4th volume of Anastasius the librarian from a Verona MS. written 1100 years ago.

Footnote 8: (return)

This new Gregorian sacramentary was carried to England by St. Augustin and the other missionaries. Mr. Palmer and after him Mr. Froude (Remains, vol. 2nd, p. 387) give a similar account of the Roman liturgy. They, like archbishop Wake, attribute the origin of the Roman, Oriental, Ethiopic and Mozarabic liturgies to St. Peter, St. James, St. Mark and St. John, and observe that all other liturgies are copied from one or other of these. "In each of these four original liturgies the eucharist is regarded as a mystery and as a sacrifice" p. 395: they all agree in the principal ceremonies of the mass, and all contain a prayer for the rest and peace of all those who have departed this life in God's faith and fear" p. 393. "Now it may be reasonably presumed", says archbishop Wake "that those passages wherein all these liturgies agree, in sense at least, if not in words, were first prescribed in the writings of the ancient fathers". See Tracts for the times, no. 63.

Footnote 9: (return)

They who wish for further details may consult Le Brun, Card. Bona, Martene, Gavant, Rock's Hierurgia etc.

Footnote 10: (return)

Because anciently sung from the *steps* of the *ambo* or pulpit, according to Rabanus Maurus an author of the 9th century, and others. In the ancient churches there were generally in the *chorus* or choir two ambones, one from which at solemn masses the lector and at a later period the subdeacon used to sing the gospel, with his face usually turned towards that side of the church, where the *men* were assembled; at Rome this was generally the south side. At low masses the missal was removed from the epistle side of the altar at the beginning of the offertory, in order to leave room for the offerings, according to an Ordinarium of Monte Casino of the year 1100. It has for a long time been customary to remove it before the gospel, which the priest recites turned towards the same direction as the deacon at high mass. Mystical meanings were afterwards assigned for this removal of the book.

Footnote 11: (return)

It is astonishing how Mr. Palmer could assert that "Leo bishop of Rome in the fifth century appears to have been the only bishop who preached in the Roman church for many Footnote: and it is said that none of his successors until the time of Pius the fifth, five hundred years afterwards, imitated his example". Orig. Liturg. vol. II, p. 59. Bingham I. IV, c. §.3. Mr. Palmer forgot all the homilies of Gregory the great, as well as the chronology of the Popes. The latter might find in the multiplicity and importance of their other occupations abundant motives for abstaining from preaching, a duty to which so many of their clergy dedicate themselves. That the early Popes however preached there can be no doubt, although most of their homilies, if ever written, have not reached our time. Not only the example of S. Peter who (whatever we may think of the local tradition of Rocca S. Pietro above Palestrina) used certainly to preach, as the Acts of the Apostles prove; but the general custom of other cities would induce the zealous Bishops of Rome to exhort and encourage their flock, particularly in time of persecution; and that at a later period they were not unaccustomed to preach is evident from the Ordo Romanus of Card. Gaetano published by Mabillon and from a Vatican MS. no. 4231, p. 197; both these documents are quoted by Cancellieri, *Descriz. delle Cappelle etc. p. 328.* See proofs that the Popes preached drawn up in chronological order in Sala's notes to Card. Bona, lib. 2. c. 7-

Footnote 12: (return)

S. Ambros. Ep. 13, serm. 34.

Footnote 13: (return)

Of the ancient offerings the following vestiges remain: candles are offered by the clergy at their ordination, bread and wine by bishops at their consecration, chalices and torches by the Roman senate on particular festivals, and in fine bread, wine, water, and, till lately, doves and other birds at the canonisation of the Saints. On the ancient offerings see Cancellieri, de Secretaries, t. I, p. 181.

Footnote 14: (return)

"This custom prevailed universally in the Christian church from the earliest period" Palmer Orig. Liturg. vol. 2, p. 75.

Footnote 15: (return)

As the ancient Roman houses had an *impluvium* in the midst of the *atrium*, so in the *atria* annexed to the Christian churches was one or more fountains (Eus. Eccl. Hist. l. X, c. 4) and sometimes a well or cistern. In these the faithful used to wash

13

their hands (Tertull. De orat. §, De lavat. man.) Thus in the atrium of St. Paul's basilica there was a cantharus, restored by Pope Leo I, of which the saint writes thus to Ennodius;

Quisque suis meritis veneranda sacraria Pauli

Ingrederis, supplex ablue fonte manus.

The *cantharus* is mentioned by Virgil Eclog. VI, 21.

Et gravis adtritâ pendebat cantharus ansa.

A large vessel of this description may be seen in the *cortili* of S. Cecilia and SS. Apostoli at Rome. It used to be blessed on the vigil or festival of the Epiphany, as it is now in the Greek and even the Roman church. When churches were built without *atria*, a vessel of blessed water was placed inside the church: in some of the older churches there is even a well. See Nibby, *Dissert. sulla forma, etc. delle antiche chiese.*

Footnote 16: (return)

See Le Brun tom. IV, diss. 15. Super usu recitandi silentio missæ partem etc. This custom was connected with the discipline of secrecy. The scripture itself does not mention what words Christ used, when He "gave thanks", before He pronounced the words of consecration; and the early church imitated this reserve. Anciently curtains concealed the altar, during the most solemn part of mass, as now in some Oriental churches. St. John Chrysostom (Hom. 3, in Ep. ad Ephes.) mentions this custom; and traces of it still remain at St. Clement's church in Rome.

Footnote 17: (return)

See ancient inscriptions from the catacombs, containing prayers for the dead in Bock's Hierurgia (vol. 2, ch. 7), also in Annali delle Scienze Religiose, Luglio 1839, as also in the well-known works on the catacombs. Bingham admits that the eucharistic sacrifice was offered for S. Augustine, S. Monica, the emperors Constantine and Valentinian at their funerals. (S. Ambrose prayed for Valentinian Gratian and Theodosius.) "In the communion service" says he "according to the custom of those times, a solemn commemoration was made of the dead in general, and prayers were offered to God for them". Bingham, Antiq. l. 23, c. 2. "The custom of praying and offering up sacrifice for the faithful departed most evidently appears to have prevailed in the church even from the time of the apostles", says the Protestant bishop Milles, Opera S. Cyrilli. p. 297. "In primitive times" says Palmer "these commemorations (in the mass) were accompanied by prayers for the departed". Origin. Liturg. vol. 2, p. 94. With these Protestant admissions before us and many others collected in the Annali delle Scienze Relig. Luglio 1839, we opine that the Rev. Mr. Breeks ought to have been solicitous for his own soul rather than for that of Mrs. Wolfrey, whose inscription was dictated by the spirit of primitive Christianity. The following is the inscription on Thorndike's tomb at Westminster "Tu lector, requiem ei et beatam in Xto resurrectionem precare". On Bp. Barrow's tomb at S. Asaph's "O vos transeuntes in domum Domini, domum orationis, orate pro conservo vestro ut inveniat requiem in die Domini". Both were written by their own direction: other Protestant testimonies may be seen ap. Srett. o. 462.

Footnote 18: (return)

Pope Vigilius (A.D. 538.) in his epistle to Profuturus, bishop of Braga in Spain, says, that the canon never varied, but that on particular festivals "we make commemoration of the holy solemnity, or of those saints whose nativities we celebrate".

Footnote 19: (return)

"The bread which we break is it not the communion of the body of Christ". 1 Cor. X, 16.

Footnote 20: (return)

This custom we may consider with Palmer as a memorial of an ancient mode of communicating under both kinds united, which is still observed in the oriental churches: Vol. 2, p. 146; or with Le Brim as a record of the practice of sending the particle to the priests of titular churches, T. 4. Micrologus and others consider this mixture as a representation of Christ's resurrection. It is very ancient, as Sala shews.

Footnote 21: (return)

"St. Paul calls the Eucharist 1 Cor. X, 16 the cup of *blessing* which *we bless.*" This incidental information vouchsafed to us in scripture, should lead us to be very cautious how we put aside other usages of the early church concerning this sacrament, which do not happen to be clearly mentioned in scripture". Tracts for the Times, Vol. 1, no. 34. The "Mass" in Cranmer's Form of prayer and administration of the Sacraments, which was declared by act of Parliament "agreable to the word of God and the primitive church" differs but little from the Roman mass above described. See Pugin's Letter on the proposed Protestant Memorial. London 1839.

Footnote 22: (return)

Macri in his Hierolexicon says, that the Cardinal kneels, to incense the Pope when seated, from respect to his *cattedra* or chair, which is the first see in the Christian church. Others say from respect to his temporal sovereignty, the archbishops of Milan are incensed with the same formality. This custom is mentioned in the 13th century by Card. Giaconio Gaetano. Ordo Romanus § 112. A certain love of proportion may have had its share in the origin of this ceremony, by which the same relative height is preserved between the Pope and the Cardinal in all cases in which the former is incensed. Thus also the assistant Bishop, who holds the Missal for the Pope, kneels when He is seated, and stands when He stands. We kneel to the Pope to receive his blessing, as we do to bishops and even priests; we also kneel from respect to his exalted dignity, not only as sovereign, but also as head of the Catholic church. It is well known that the British peers kneel even to the empty throne of their sovereign. Kneeling is a very ancient token of profound respect; it was paid to Joseph in Egypt, Gen. XLI, 43; to Elias, 4 Kings I, 13 etc.

Footnote 23: (return)

"O that an angel" says St. Ambrose, "would appear to us also, when incensing the altar, and offering sacrifice". Expl. in. Luc. l. 1, c. 25, n. 9.

Footnote 24: (return)

Incense is, as we shall see in c. 2; an emblem of prayer, and in this sense it is offered to the B. Sacrament, to Christ represented by the crucifix, and adored on the altar. The gospel is incensed to signify the sweet odour which it communicates to our souls; and the ministers of God, to signify, according to St. Thomas, that God maketh manifest *the odour* of his knowledge by us in every place: "For we are unto God *the good odour* of Christ in them who are saved, and in them who perish". 2 Cor. II, 14, 15. In fine the bread and wine offered to God are incensed to signify the spices with which the body of Christ was embalmed in the tomb; such at least is the explanation given in the Liturgy of St. Chrysostom; and it is from the oriental churches that the Latin church has taken this last practice. Incense is a token of respect in these and other cases.

Footnote 25: (return)

A taper with a stand, called a *bugia*, is held at divine service for persons in ecclesiastical dignity, as a sign of distinction, and to throw additional light on the book from which they read. The taper held for the Pope at the *cappelle* has no stand, and is enkindled from a light concealed within the desk, on which the assistant Bishop places the missal. This is a memorial of an ancient monastic custom mentioned by Martene Lib. 1, De rit. Eccl. p. 277, 232.

CHAP. II.

ON THE CEREMONIES OF PALM-SUNDAY

CONTENTS.

Part 1. *Introductory*. Mysteries and devotion of holy-week—Palm-Sunday, entry of Christ into Jerusalem—of Julius II into Rome—Sixtus V and Captain Bresca—triumphant return of Pius VII to Rome, contrasted with ancient Roman triumphs. Part 2. *Descriptive*, Palm-sunday—lights used at mass etc.—vestments—*ubbidienza*, blessing of the palms, benedictions, holy water, incense—distribution of the palms—order in which the prelates and others receive them—solemn procession with palms, *sedia gestatoria*—ceremonies peculiar to this procession—its antiquity—High mass, its peculiar ceremonies on palm-sunday—Passio—Cardinal great Penitentiary at S. John Lateran's.

"Hosanna to the son of David: blessed is he that cometh in the name of the Lord, Hosanna in the highest". Matt. XXI, 9.

|P. I. Holy-week

The sufferings and death of Jesus Christ are the mysteries which the catholic church commemorates during holy week. "On these days" says S. John Chrysostom (in Ps. CXCIV) "was the tyranny of the devil overthrown, sin and its curse were taken away, heaven was opened and made accessible". It was then becoming that christians should consecrate these days of mercy, of grace and salvation to exercises of penance, devotion, and thanksgiving. The imposing liturgy of the Roman church is at this season more than usually solemn; and it is our task to describe, and endeavour to trace to their origin, its varied ceremonies.

|Palm-Sunday, Christ's entry into Jerusalem.

Palm-sunday is so called from the commemoration of our blessed Saviour's entry into Jerusalem, when, according to St. John (XII, 13) "a great multitude took branches of palm-trees, and went forth to meet him, and cried: "Hosanna, blessed is he that cometh in the name of the Lord". Thus when Simon Maccabee subdued Jerusalem, he entered it "with thanksgiving and branches of palm-trees, and harps, and cymbals, and hymns and canticles, because the great enemy was destroyed out of Israel". 1 Macc. XIII. The entry of our divine Redeemer therefore was one of triumph: but it was also the

17

entry of a king into his capital: for "many spread their garments in the way" (Mark XI, 8), as when Jehu was elected king, (4 Kings IX, 13), the Israelites spread their garments under his feet. Thus also Plutarch relates of Cato of Utica, that the soldiers regretting the expiration of his authority with many tears and embraces spread their garments, where he passed on foot.

Pope Julius II returning to Rome after the siege of Mirandola distributed palms to the Roman court at S. Maria del Popolo; and then rode in triumphal procession to the Vatican passing under seven arches adorned with representations of his extraordinary and heroic deeds[26].

Sixtus V and Captain Bresca.

When Sixtus V. undertook to erect in the Piazza di San Pietro the ponderous egyptian obelisk[27], which formerly adorned Nero's circus at the Vatican, he forbade on pain of death that any one should speak lest the attention of the workmen should be taken off from their arduous task. A naval officer of S. Remo, who happened to be present, foreseeing that the ropes would take fire, cried out "*acqua alle funi*". He was immediately arrested by the Swiss guards, as we see him represented in the small fresco in the Vatican library, and was conducted before the Pontiff. Sixtus shewed that his severity was based on justice; for instead of punishing the transgressor of his orders, he offered him the choice of his own reward. They who have observed the great abundance of palms which grow in the neighbourhood of S. Remo, on the coast between Nice and Genoa, will not be surprised to hear, that the first wish of the gallant captain was to enjoy the privilege of supplying the pontifical chapel with palms. The Pope granted him this exclusive right and it is still enjoyed by one of his family.

Return of Pius VII to Rome.

When the meek and benevolent Pius VII was returning to Rome from exile and captivity, Dr. Bresca, one of the captain's descendants, contrived, though not without great risk, to convey to Rome the choicest palms of S. Remo and Bordighera. At the house of his friend Viale half a mile outside the Porta del Popolo, he assembled twenty five *orfanelli* dressed in their white cassocks, and forty-five *verginelle*. When the carriage of the beloved Pontiff approached, this double choir of children appeared, bearing palms in their hands and singing joyous canticles of benediction but I must describe this lovely scene in the melodious language of the south. "Ciascuno di essi (says Cancellieri) recava in mano una di queste palme di color d'oro altissime e cadenti come tante vaghissime piume. Sei zitelle sostenevano de'galanti panieri di freschissimi fiori pendenti dal loro collo, con nastri bianchi e gialli, relativi allo stendardo Pontificio. Quindi tutti si schierarono in buon ordine sulle due ale delta strada, e mentre le ragazze versavano graziosamente a mani piene da' loro canestrelli la verzura ed i fiori, quella selva ondeggiante di palme, tributate al trionfo del S. Padre dal candore e dall' innocenza, sorprese con la novità di uno spettacolo, che non potè a meno d'intenerire, e di muovere tutti gli astanti".

If we now look back for a moment to the triumphs of the pagan emperors, well may we bless God for the change which the religion of Christ has wrought in this city. After they had let loose war, and famine, and pestilence, to prey upon hapless nations, they ascended the Capitol to offer incense with polluted hands to their profane gods; and meantime the groans of the dying and unpitied princes, whom they had reserved to decorate their triumph, ascended from the scala Gemonia to call down the vengeance of heaven upon their oppressors. But while the pacific and holy vicar of Christ returns in triumph to his capital, the lips of babes and sucklings sing his praises, as they did those of his Divine Master, and he implores heaven to shower down benedictions on his enemies as well as his beloved children.

P. II Papal chapel on palm-sunday.

Lights used at mass, etc.

At about 9 o'clock on palm-sunday morning the Cardinals, Prelates and others assemble near the chapel of the Pieta at S. Peter's, as at present the solemn service takes place in that basilica, and not as formerly in the Sixtine chapel. The crucifix over the altar is veiled, in token of the mourning of the church over her divine spouse's sufferings[28]. On the altar are six lighted candles, and other torches are brought in after the *Sanctus* of the Mass, and held till after the elevation, in honour of the B. Sacrament, by four *acoliti ceroferarii*[29].

sacred vestments

As the pope is to bless and distribute the palms, and a solemn procession is to take place, the Cardinals put on their sacred vestments, viz. all of them the amice, the cardinal bishops the surplice and the cope, the priests the chasuble, and the deacons a chasuble shorter in front than that of the priests. The auditors of the Rota, *Cherici di Camera, Votanti*, and *Abbreviatori* put on a *cotta* or supplice. The bishops and mitred abbots wear the cope, and the *Penitenzieri* or confessors of St. Peter's, the chasuble. The copes of the cardinal bishops are ornamented with a *formale*, adorned with three large bosses or projections of pearls arranged in a perpendicular line, while the Pope's are in a triangular order, evidently alluding, to the blessed Trinity. As this is a day of mourning, the sacred vestments are purple.

ubbidienza.

Thus attired and holding their mitres the Cardinals remain standing while the

Pope is vested by the assistant Cardinal-deacons who put on His Holiness the amice, alb, girdle, stole, red cope, *formale* or clasp, and mitre. All then move in procession towards the high-altar in the order observed in the procession of the palms, as described below:[30] the Pope descends from His *sedia gestatoria* to adore the Holy Sacrament with the Cardinals etc. The procession then goes to the high-altar; and having prayed for a short time before it, the Pope goes to the throne,[31] and there receives the *ubbidienza* or homage of all the cardinals present, who in turn kiss His right hand covered with the cope. This ceremony which takes place at all solemn offices, except on good friday, and at masses for the dead, bears some resemblance to the old homage of feudal times[32].

Blessing of the palms.

Some palms are arranged on the altar. The Pope's chief Sacristan, who is a bishop chosen from the Augustinian order bears one, and kneels on the steps of the throne between the deacon and subdeacon, who bear two larger palms. His Holiness reads the usual prayers over the palms, sprinkles them with holy water, and incenses them three times.

Distribution of the palms.

When the palms have been blessed[33], the Cardinal Dean receives from the governor of Rome and presents to the Pope those three palms, which were borne by *M. Sagrista*, the deacon and subdeacon. One of these is held during the service by the prince assistant at the throne, the other two are delivered to the care of *M. Coppiere*, one of the *Camerieri segreti partecipanti*: the shortest is carried by the Pope in the procession. An embroidered apron is now placed over the Pope's knees, and the cardinals in turn receive a palm from Him, kissing the palm, his right hand and knee. The bishops present kiss the palm which they receive and his right knee: and the mitred abbots and *Penitenzieri* kiss the palm and his foot[34], as do all who come after them in the following order, which is observed also on good-friday at the kissing of the cross, and it is also on candlemas-day and ash-wednesday.

The Governor, the Prince assistant, the *Uditore della Camera*, the Treasurer, the *Maggiordomo*, the Apostolic protonotaries; the Generals of Religious Orders, the *Conservatori* and Prior of the *Caporioni*, the *Maestro del S. Ospizio*, the *Uditori di Rota*, the *Maestro del S. Palazzo*, the *Votanti di Segnatura*, the *Abbreviatori del Parco maggiore*, the priest, deacon, and subdeacon who assist the cardinal who is to celebrate mass, the Masters of ceremonies, the *Camerieri segreti* and *d'onore*, the Consistorial advocates, the *Cappellani segreti*, *d'onore* and *comuni*, the *Ajutanti di camera*, the *bussolanti*, the *Procuratori generali* of religious orders, the *Procuratori di Collegio*, the singers, the clerks of the papal chapel, the cardinal's *caudatarii*, the *ostiarii*, the mace-bearers, some students of the German college, and in fine such noblemen and gentlemen as are admitted on this occasion to receive a palm from His Holiness, who is assisted as usual by two Card. deacons.

During the distribution of the palms, the anthems *Pueri Hebrœorum* etc. are sung by the choir; and when it is finished, the Pope washes His hands, and says the usual concluding prayer: the prince stationed at the throne brings the water, and the Cardinal Dean presents the towel to His Holiness.

|*Solemn procession.*

The Pope then puts incense into the thurible for the procession, and the first Card. Deacon turning towards the people says according to the old formula Let us proceed in peace: the choir answers, in the name of Christ. Amen'. The procession, in which the blessed palms are carried, moves round S. Peter's, in the following order, which is observed also for the most part on holy thursday and good friday. The *Procuratori di Collegio*,[35] *Procuratori generali*, the *Bussolanti*, the *Ajutanti di Camera*, *Cappellani comuni* and *segreti*, the Consistorial advocates, the *Camerieri d' onore*, and *segreti*, the singers, the *Abbreviatori, Votanti di Segnatura, Cherici di Camera, Uditori di Rota*, the Thurifer, (*Votante di Segnatura*), the Subdeacon (*Uditore di Rota*) who carries the cross ornamented with a small palm, between two acolythes (*Votanti di Segnatura*) carrying candles, the *Penitenzieri*, the mitred abbots, bishops and the Cardinal deacons, priests and bishops all wearing their mitres.[36] The Pope is preceded by many officers of his guards (who go to the throne towards the end of the distribution of palms), the *Maestro del S. Ospizio*, the *Conservatori*, Senator and Governor of Rome. His Holiness is carried on his *Sedia gestatoria*[37] under a canopy supported by 8 *Referendarii* (prelates of the tribunal of *Segnatura*) between the *flabelli* carried by two of His *Camerieri*. He is followed by the dean of the Rota (whose duty it is to bear His mitre) between two *camerieri segreti* (who as well as two Auditors of the Rota bear His train when occasion requires), by the *Uditore della Camera*, the Treasurer, *Maggiordomo*, Protonotaries and Generals of religious orders.

During the procession the choir sings the anthem, *Cum appropinquaret etc.* When the procession is in the portico, two soprano singers reenter the basilica, and shut the door: then turning towards the door, they sing the first verse of the hymn *Gloria, laus et honor*[38] and the other verses alternately with the choir, which remains without. The subdeacon knocks at the gate with the cross, and it is immediately opened; the procession returns into the church, and the choir sings the concluding anthems.

|*its antiquity.*

The solemn commemoration, which we have described, of Christ's triumphant entry into Jerusalem, could never have taken place during times of persecution: nor did it originate immediately after Constantine had ensured peace to the church. Martene (De ant. Eccl. Rit. lib. IV, c. 20) could find no mention of it before the 8th or 9th century, when Amalarius says "In memory of this we are accustomed to carry palm-branches, and cry Hosanna". Merati however, in his notes to Gavant, considers that he has found traces of it in the Gregorian and Gelasian sacramentaries, and in a Roman calendar of the beginning of the fifth century[39] and his opinion is adopted by Benedict XIV. The ceremonies of the church of Jerusalem on this day were a still closer imitation of the entry of Christ into that city.

When the procession is ended, the cardinals, bishops, and mitred abbots take off their sacred vestments and the prelates their surplices, and they all resume their respective *cappe*; the *Penitenzieri* retire, and mass is celebrated by a cardinal of the order of priests. Having already given an account not only of low mass, but also of the additional ceremonies of high mass, as celebrated in the papal chapel, we shall here mention those only which are peculiar to palm-sunday.

At those words of the epistle (which is sung as usual by the subdeacon), "in the name of Jesus let every knee bow", the whole assembly kneels to adore their divine Redeemer, who became obedient unto death for our salvation. The affecting account of His sufferings and death is then sung by three priests[40] belonging to the pontifical choir, and habited as deacons in alb and stole. The history itself is sung by a tenor voice, the words, of our Saviour by a bass, and those of any other single voice by a *contralto*, called the *ancilla*, as he sings the words of the *maid* to S. Peter: the choir sings the words of the multitude[41]. The church, mourning over the sufferings of her divine Spouse, does not allow the incense, lights, or the benediction and salutation usual before the gospel; but the palms are borne to signify the triumphs consequent on His death as they are also from the elevation till after the communion. All stand up as usual from respect to the holy gospel ("as servants before their Lord" Amalarius) but kneel for a short time at the words "Jesus crying with a loud voice yielded up the ghost", to adore that God of love who died for mankind. The latter part of the gospel is sung in the usual chant by the deacon, but without the customary lights[42]. At the offertory is sung the first part of the beautiful hymn *Stabat Mater*: the music is Palestrina's, and is justly and highly panegyrised by Baini; it has been published by Dr. Burney. Both the *introit* and communion are sung without, and the offertory with, counterpoint: the *Kyrie eleison*, Gradual and tract, in plain chant. The Benedictus qui venit is usually very beautiful. At the end of the mass, as there has been no sermon, the Card. celebrant announces from the altar the Pope's usual grant to all present of an indulgence[43] or remission of the *temporal* punishment due for past sins, whose guilt has been already remitted.

When the mass is ended, the palms are carried home by those who have received them, and are preserved with respect. Two larger than the rest are kept until the ascension, in the sacristy called the *Letto dei Paramenti* because anciently the aged Pontiffs after their fatiguing walk to the stational churches used to repose on a *letto* or bed prepared for them in the sacristy, where they afterwards put on the *paramenti* or vestments. The paschal candle also, an emblem of Christ the true light, as we shall afterwards see is removed on the day of the ascension: this circumstance may explain the above-mentioned custom.

Cardinal penitentiary at S. John Lateran's.

In the afternoon of palm-sunday, the Cardinal great Penitentiary goes in state to S. John Lateran's. He is met, before he enters their college, by the minor penitentiaries, who at this basilic are Franciscans, *minori osservanti*. Having sprinkled those present with holy water, he goes up to their private oratory[44] in the Lateran palace, whither he is escorted by the prelates and other ministers of the apostolic *Penitenzieria*. After a short prayer, he proceeds to the library, where he holds the *Segnatura* or tribunal for signing documents relating to his office, and afterwards enters the basilic of St. John Lateran's, where he is received by four canons. Here seated at his tribunal of penance, he touches with his rod the heads of the prelates, ministers and others who approach to him; and for this act of humiliation they receive an indulgence, or remission of the canonical penance, of 100 days. He also hears the confessions of any persons who may choose to present themselves: but the solution of difficult cases and absolution from crimes reserved to his jurisdiction may be obtained without confessing to his Eminence on so public an occasion[45].

The ceremonies, which we have described, are designed to honour our divine Redeemer, whose actions and sufferings are thereby commemorated, and at the same time to excite sentiments of devotion in the hearts of His servants. Here ought the catholic to exercise faith, hope, love, and contrition for his sins: and *all*, of whatever country or creed they may be, who are admitted with hospitality and liberality to witness the solemn and imposing service, if they do not feel such noble sentiments, ought at least to observe that external decorum, which the season, the place, the hierarchy, and above all the commemoration of the sufferings of the God of charity will dictate to every well-educated and well-principled mind. It is to be lamented, that not only the devotion of Catholics is disturbed, but their feelings also are occasionally insulted in their own house of worship by the unbecoming remarks of individuals—but enough: "you have not so learned Christ: if yet you have heard him, and have been taught in him, as the truth is in Jesus". Ephes. IV, 20, 21. If on this day even the inhabitants of Jerusalem received Him with triumph and jubilee, let us His disciples and children offer to Him the best tribute in our power of love praise and adoration.

Footnote 26: (return)

See Cancellieri, *Solenni possessi de'Papi, p.* 539.

Footnote 27: (return)

According to Champollion, it was originally erected in Heliopolis by Ramesses 7th son of the great Ramesses or Sesostris; Pliny says by Nuncoreus son of Sesostris. Caligula transported it to Rome, and placed it in the circus afterwards called Nero's, where it remained standing till the time of Sixtus V.

Footnote 28: (return)

It was customary in Lent, says St. Audoenus, to cover with a linen veil the tomb of Eligius to conceal the brightness of the gold and the splendour of the gems". Vita S. Eligii l. 2. c. 40. Thus does the church at this season put off her costly nuptial robes, and vest herself in weeds of deepest mourning. The time for veiling the crucifix and images has varied at different periods. The Saturday before passion-sunday is now the first, and holy Saturday the last day, of this observance.

Footnote 29: (return)

S. Isidore (A.D. 600.) observes, that acolythes are called in Latin *Ceroferarii* "from their carrying wax tapers when the gospel is to be read or sacrifice is to be offered". In the eleventh century Micrologus testifies "that Mass, according to the *Ordo Romanus,* was never celebrated without lights, even in the day time, as a type of the light of Christ". To this custom we shall recur in the following chapter.

Footnote 30: (return)

Pietro de Marca maintains, that the crucifix borne before the Pope was substituted in place of the *labarum* or standard carried before the emperors. That of Constantine had the form of a cross, and was surmounted with XP the first letters of Christ's name, Eus. In Vita Const. l. 4.

Footnote 31: (return)

I shall not speak of some ancient ceremonies of holy week which have fallen into disuse, such as the custom of carrying the gospel or the B. Sacrament in triumphant procession on Palm-Sunday, and others alluded to by Cancellieri and described by Martene, De Antiq. Eccl. Rit.

Footnote 32: (return)

In times of schism caused by antipopes it was a practice of the utmost importance. Thus we read in Baronius' Annals A.D. 1160, that when the antipope Cardinal Octavianus, who assumed the name of Victor, had been illegitimately elected, the chapter of St. Peter's came immediately to the feet of the said Pope Victor, and *obeyed* "obedivit" and the clergy and people paid due reverence to him, and a great multitude in like manner *obeyed*: "the rectors also came to his feet, and paid *obedience* and reverence". Then follows a long list of the clergy of various Roman churches, all of whom it is said that they *obeyed.* Thus,

"The Lateran prior and his canons *obeyed.* The clergy of the patriarchal church of S. Mary Major's *obeyed* etc."

This *obedience* was evidently an external sign of their acknowledging Victor as Pope in place of Alexander, the legitimate pontiff. Anciently the Pope received the homage of the deacons in the sacristy; they afterwards went out of the sacristy to put on their dalmatics. Cancellieri de Secretariis T.I. In the sacristy the Pope gave the *peace* to the Bishops, Cardinals, Prefect, Senator, and other lay princes according to the canon Benedict, Cencius Camerarius and Cajetan. The ordines Romani mention the bowing of the Subdeacon at the knees of the Pontiff, and the kissing of his hand by the priests, the archdeacon and secundarius De secretariis T. I, p. 409.

Footnote 33: (return)

Many forms of benediction of persons and things taken from ancient Pontificals and manuscript rituals may be seen in Martene, De antiquis Ecclesiae Ritibus. The church generally uses holy-water and incense when blessing God's creatures, which are "sanctified by the word of God and prayer" 1 Tom. IV, 5. God had appointed water of expiation to be used by the Jews, Numbers XIX. Lustral water used to be sprinkled also by the Pagans; Terque senem flamma, ter aqua, ter sulphure purget. Ov. Met. l. 7. Anastasius says that Alexander I, who was Pope in 108 "appointed that water for sprinkling should be blessed with salt in private houses." It is mentioned also in the apostolic constitutions. Boldetti in his *Cemeterii de' martiri* notices the short columns supporting small vases, in corners of the chapels in the catacombs; and Bottari has published and illustrated in his *Roma sotterranea* an interesting fresco discovered in the catacombs of S. Agnese, and representing five figures carrying vessels closely resembling those still used for holy water; four of those figures carry branches supposed to be of the palm-tree: the fifth holds an aspergillum with which holy water is still sprinkled. A copy of this fresco may be seen also in Rock's Hierurgia, p. 668. Incense is a symbol of prayers. "Let my prayer, O Lord" we say with the Psalmist "be directed as incense in thy sight". God had appointed it to be used in the Jewish worship, and St. John says, that an "angel came and stood before the altar, having a golden censer, and there was given to him much incense, that he should offer of the prayers of all the saints upon the golden altar, which is before the throne of God: and the smoke of the incense of the prayers of the saints ascended up before God, from the hand of the angel". Apoc. VIII, 3, 5. Of the apostolic antiquity of its use the Protestant bishop Beveridge adduces proofs in his Vindication of the apostolical canons. The ancient liturgies of the east and west agree in prescribing the use of incense, and in particular at the beginning of mass, at the offertory etc. See Renaudot, Assemani, Le Brun etc. Constantine, according to Anastasius in his life of S. Silvester, gave two golden thuribles to the Lateran basilis, and a third adorned with jewels to the Baptistery. See Card. Bona, Rerum Liturgicarum lib. I, c. XXV, § 9.

Footnote 34: (return)

Of the antiquity of the custom of kissing the Pope's foot we have proofs in Anastasius the librarian in the lives of Popes Constantine and Leo IV. When Valentine was elected Pope in 827, his feet were kissed by the Roman senate and people at S. John Lateran's. Numerous instances also are on record of sovereigns who have kissed the feet of the Popes, and Pouyard has written a dissertation to shew, that this custom was anterior to that of marking the papal shoes or sandals with a cross. This token of profound respect was given also to the emperors of the east at Byzantium.

Footnote 35: (return)

These are distinguished lawyers habited in black *cappe*. For an account of the various offices above-mentioned and of their origin see The Papal Chapel, Described etc. by C.M. Baggs. Rome. 1839.

Footnote 36: (return)

That crosses, candles and incense were anciently used in processions appears from S. Gregory of Tours, de Vit. Patrum, c. 13.

Footnote 37: (return)

The kings and chief magistrates of ancient Rome were entitled to a *sella curulis*, or chair of state, which used to be placed in their chariots. Gell. III; 18. They were seated on it also at their tribunal on solemn occasions. Virgil makes old king Latinus say:

Et *sellam regni* trabeamque *insignia nostri. Æn.* XI. 334. The Romans had borrowed it from the Etruscans according to Dionysius of Halicarnassus. (Clement of Alexandria observes, That many of the rites of Etruria were imported from Asia; and Diodorus (lib. 5.) represents these insignia as derived from Lydia. See Phoebens. De Identitate Cathedræ S. Petri p. XX. seq.) It was richly adorned, *conspicuum signis*, according to Ovid, Pont. IV. 5, 18. In the Pope's carriage even now there is a chair of state, and to Him alone is reserved the honour of a *sedia gestatoria*. Pope Stephen II in 751 was carried to the basilica of Constantine on the shoulders of the Romans exulting at his election: and from this fact some derive the custom of carrying the Pope in His chair on solemn occasions.

Footnote 38: (return)

This hymn is attributed to the abbot Theodulph afterwards bishop of Orleans, who lived in the 9th century. If it were true, that he sang it as the emperor Louis le debonnaire was passing by the prison, in which he was confined, and that he was in consequence liberated, we should have a historical reason for the shutting and opening of the door, and for the hymn's being sung partly inside the church. This account has however been called in question by Menard, Macri, Martene and others; and hence Pouget, and after him Benedict XIV and others are contented with a mystic reason for such ceremonies, viz, that heaven was closed to man in consequence of sin, and was opened to him by the cross of Christ.

Footnote 39: (return)

In these it is called Dominica ad Palmas, Dominica in Palmis, and in the Gregorian Sacramentary mention is made, in the prayer which precedes communion, of the faithful carrying palm-branches.

Footnote 40: (return)

Anciently a cardinal deacon used to read it, and to sing only the words "Eli, Eli, lamma sabachthani".

Footnote 41: (return)

The author of this exquisite chant is unknown: Baini supposes that he was a member of the pontifical choir: it has been sung in the papal chapel since the middle of the 13th century. In 1585 it, together with the rest of the service of holy week, was published by Tommaso da Vittoria with the words of the people harmonised for 4 and 5 voices; his method was adopted by the papal choir, which adorns it with many traditional graces, and in particular gives occasionally, says Baini, to the words of the multitude "the irresistible force of a most robust harmony". The abbate Alfieri has published a new edition of the *Passios*.

Footnote 42: (return)

In Africa till the time of S. Augustine, the Passion used to be read in holy week from the gospel of S. Matthew alone; but by his direction, as he mentions in his 232nd discourse, it was read every year from all the four evangelists; and this custom is still observed.

That God, after He has pardoned sin and consequently remitted its eternal punishment, often, if not generally, demands temporal satisfaction from the sinner, is evident from many instances in scripture, such as those of David (2 Sam. XII) of Moses (Deuteron. XXXII compare Num. XIV) to say nothing of Adam (Gen. III) and all his posterity, who endure the temporal punishment of original sin, even when its stain has been washed away by baptism. Now the church by virtue of the ample authority with which Christ has invested her (Matt. XVIII, John XX) and in particular her chief pastor (Matt. XVI) has from the beginning exercised the power of remitting the temporal punishment of actual sins. Thus S. Paul pardoned the incestuous Corinthian (2. Cor. II): in times of persecution the bishops at the request of the martyrs remitted the penance imposed on those who had fallen into idolatry (Tersul. lib. ad martyres, Euseb. Hist. Eccl. lib. V, c. 4. S. Cyprian. Epist. XIII etc.), to say nothing of canons of the 4th century which prescribe that indulgences should be granted to *fervent* penitents, of the crusades, and of the indulgences granted to those who contributed money for the building of S. Peter's, etc. Indulgences presuppose repentance and confession, and the performance of those good works which are prescribed as conditions necessary for their acquisition, as communion, prayers, alms etc.

Footnote 44: (return)

It was built by Calixtus II, and was for two centuries and a half the Vestry of the Roman Pontiffs. It was repaired and consecrated in 1747. See Cancellieri. De Secretariis T. I, p. 342.

Footnote 45: (return)

In the third century, in the time of Pope Cornelius there were priests appointed to absolve those who had fallen into idolatry; and they were called *Presbyteri Pænitentium*. S. Marcellus also, according to Anastasius, after the persecution raised by Diocletian, appointed in Rome titular churches, in which penance as well as baptism were administered by priests, the former sacrament is conferred by the minor penitentiaries. Pope Simplicius in fine, as we learn from the same author, destined fixed weeks at S. Peter's, S. Paul's, and S. Laurence's, to *receive penitents* and administer baptism. From the usual custom of Rome in such matters, Zaccaria argues that during the first five or six centuries, according to the general custom proved by Thomassin, the great penitentiary was the *bishop himself of the city* in which they resided. It is however certain, that in the 4th century from the numerous priests of Constantinople one was selected called a penitentiary, who took cognisance of crimes, to which public penance was annexed by the canons. At Rome also there was a cardinal penitentiary long before the fourth council of Lateran, which in 1215 prescribed that bishops should appoint penitentiaries, for Berthod priest of Constance relates in his chronicle, that in the year 1084 he was promoted to the dignity of cardinal-priest and penitentiary of the Roman church.

CHAP III.

ON THE DIVINE OFFICE, AND THE OFFICE OF TENEBRAE IN PARTICULAR.

CONTENTS.

PART 1. *Introductory*. Breviary—Divine office, its origin—performed by the early Christians—ancient and modern editions of the breviary. PART 2. *Descriptive*. Office of Tenebræ—Matins and Lauds—extinction of the lights—meaning of this ceremony—chant, lamentations—conclusions of the office—*Miserere*, its music—Card. Penitentiary at S. Mary Major's. *Trinità dei Pellegrini.*

"*I will bless the Lord at all times: his praise shall always be in my mouth*". Ps. XXXIII, 2.

"*He humbled himself, becoming obedient unto death, even the death of the cross*". Phil. II, 8.

|*P. I. Breviary.*

We shall not hesitate to borrow the following account of the church office contained in the Roman Breviary from a Protestant divine (Tracts of the Times no. 75). "The word *Breviarum* first occurs in the work of an author of the eleventh century (Micrologus) and it is used to denote a compendium or systematic arrangement of the devotional offices of the church. Till that time they were contained in several independent volumes, according to the nature of each. Such, for instance, were the *Psalteria, Homilaria, Hymnaria*, and the like, to be used in the service in due course. But at his memorable era, and under the auspices of the Pontiff who makes it memorable, Gregory VII, an Order was drawn up, for the use of the Roman church, containing in one all these different collections, introducing the separate members of each in its proper place, and harmonising them together by the use of rubrics.

|*Divine office, its origin.*

"Gregory VII did but restore and harmonise these offices; which seem to have existed more or less the same in constituent parts, though not in order and system, from Apostolic times. In their present shape they are appointed for seven distinct seasons in the twenty four hours, and consist of prayers, praises and thanksgivings of various forms; and, as regards both contents and hours, are the continuation of a system of worship observed by the Apostles and their converts. As to *contents*, the Breviary service consists of the Psalms; of Hymns and Canticles; of Lessons and Texts from inspired and Ecclesiastical authors; of Antiphons, Verses and Responses, and Sentences; and of Collects. And analogous to this seems to have been the usage of the Corinthian Christians, whom St. Paul blames for refusing to agree in some common order of worship, when they came together, *every one of them* having a Psalm, or a doctrine, a tongue, a revelation, an interpretation (1 Cor. XIV, 26). On the other hand, the catholic *seasons* of devotion are certainly derived from apostolic usage. The Jewish observance of the third, sixth and ninth hours for prayer, was continued by the inspired founders of the Christian church. What Daniel had practised, even when the decree was signed forbidding it, *"kneeling on his knees three times a day, and praying and giving thanks unto his God"*, S. Peter and the other Apostles were solicitous in preserving. It was when *"they were all with one accord in one place"*, at "the *third* hour of the day", that the Holy Ghost came down upon them at Pentecost. It was at the *sixth* hour, that St. Peter "went up upon the house-top to pray" and saw the vision revealing to him the admission of the gentiles into church. And it was at the *ninth* hour that "Peter and John went up together into the temple", being "the hour of prayer". But though these were the more remarkable seasons of devotion, there certainly were others besides them in the first age of the church. After our Saviour's departure, the Apostles, we are informed, "all *continued* with one accord in prayer and supplication, with the women, and Mary the mother of Jesus, and with His brethren": and with this accords the repealed exhortation to pray together without ceasing, which occurs in St. Paul's epistles. It will be observed that he insists in one passage on prayer to the abridgment of sleep (Eph. VI, 18); and one recorded passage of his life exemplifies his precept: "And at midnight Paul and Silas prayed, and sang praises unto God, and the prisoners heard them".

In subsequent times the Hours of prayer were gradually developed from the three, or (with midnight) the four seasons above enumerated, to seven, viz. by the addition of Prime (the first hour), Vespers (the evening), and Compline (bedtime); according to the words of the Psalm, "Seven times a day do I praise Thee, because of Thy righteous judgment. Other pious and instructive reasons existed, or have since been perceived for this number".[46] Thus far our Protestant author, with whose remarks we are too well pleased to go out of our way to dispute with him the truth of some other portions of his tract, which are objectionable.

|Performed by the early Christians.

That the early Christians continued after the time of the apostles to observe the hours of prayer above enumerated is proved by Martene (De Ant. Eccl.

Rit. T. 3) who has collected many decisive passages from the Greek and Latin Fathers. We shall content ourselves with one taken from a work on prayer by S. Cyprian, bishop of Carthage in the third century. Having mentioned Daniel's practice of praying three times a day, he observes, that it is manifest that there was something mysterious or symbolical in the ancient practice. "For the holy Ghost descended on the disciples at the third hour; at the sixth hour Peter going to the house-top was instructed by God to admit all to the grace of salvation; and the Lord, who was crucified at the sixth hour, washed away our sins with his blood at the ninth hour, and completed the victory by his passion. For us however, besides the hours anciently observed, the times and also the symbols of prayer have increased. For we must pray in the morning, to celebrate the resurrection of the Lord; also when the sun recedes and the day ceases; for Christ is the true sun and the true day, and when we pray that the light of Christ may again come upon us, we pray that his coming may impart to us the grace of eternal light: and let us who are always in Christ, that is, in the light, not cease from prayer at night". See also Dr. Cave's Primitive Christianity Part. 1, c. 9.

|*Editions of the breviary.*

"The old Roman breviary" says the author of Tract 75 above quoted "had long before Gregory VII's time been received in various parts of Europe; and in England since the time of Gregory the great who after the pattern of Leo and Gelasius before him had been a reformer of it". The people used anciently to join with the clergy in offering this, constant tribute of praise to God; but the duty of daily reciting it is obligatory only upon the Catholic clergy, and religious orders. S. Benedict shortened it considerably, (as Grancolas observes, Com. Hist. in Brev. Rom.) New editions and emendations of it were published successively by the authority of St. Gregory VII, Nicholas III, and Clement VII, and finally the Roman Breviary at present used was restored by order of the Council of Trent, published by Pope Pius V, and revised by Clement VIII, and Urban VIII. It follows closely, as Merati observes, that first adopted by the regular-clerks in the 16th century, and resembles the edition published by Haymo, general of the Franciscans, and authorised by Nicholas III (A.D. 1278). Hence it is called by the author of Tract 75 the *Franciscan* Breviary. It is however founded upon the old Roman Breviary, which the Franciscans by the direction of their holy founder had adopted: for according to Rodolfo, dean of Tongres Cap. XXII, when the Popes dwelt at the Lateran, the *office of the Papal chapel* was much shorter than that of the other churches of Rome; it was composed by Innocent III, and was adopted by the Franciscans instituted at his time. Nicolas III ordered that all the Roman churches should use the Franciscan Breviary as reformed by Haymo, in 1241. "Our own daily service", says the above-mentioned minister of the church of

England is confessedly formed upon the Breviary".

P. II. Office of Tenebræ.

Having premised thus much on the office in general, we may now return to holy-week. Besides palm-sunday, three other days in the week are particularly devoted to the commemoration of the history of our redemption; holy-thursday, because on it our Lord instituted the blessed Eucharist, and his passion began; good-friday, on which He was crucified and died; and holy saturday, on which His sacred body remained in the tomb. The church commences her solemn service of each of these days with that part of the divine office called matins and lauds, and at this time Tenebrae from the *darkness* with which it concludes. It used of old to be celebrated at night, as it still is by some religious communities[47]; but it now takes place on the afternoon preceding each of those three days. Nor is this unusual: for "the ecclesiastical day is considered to begin with the evening or Vesper service, according to the Jewish reckoning, as alluded to in the text. "In the evening and morning and at noon day will I pray, and that instantly". (Tracts of the Times, No. 75).

Matins and Lauds.

The office of Matin so called from Matuta or Aurora consists at Tenebræ of three *nocturns*. Each of these is composed of three appropriate psalms with their anthems, followed by three lessons taken from scripture or the fathers. Immediately after matins, Lauds or the praises of God are sung: they consist of five psalms besides the *Benedictus* or canticle of Zachary, to which succeeds the *Miserere* or 50th psalm. Some of the short prayers usually said are omitted: for the church during this season of mourning strips her liturgy as well as her altars of their usual ornaments[48].

Extinction of the lights.

A triangular candlestick, upon which are placed fifteen candles, corresponding to the number of psalms recited before the *Miserere*, is peculiar to this solemn office, and is placed at the epistle-side of the altar. After each psalm one of the candles is extinguished by a Master of ceremonies, and after the *Benedictus* the candle placed on the top of the triangular candlestick is not extinguished, but is concealed behind the altar and brought out at the end of the service; while that canticle is sung, the six candles on the altar also are extinguished, as well as those above the *cancellata* or rails[49].

Meaning of this ceremony.

Lamps and candelabra were presented to the sanctuary by the faithful during the first ages of persecution; and in more tranquil times to the basilicas by Constantine and others who erected or dedicated them. They were lighted, as

S. Jerome observes, in the day time "not to drive away darkness, but as a sign of joy": and therefore the custom of gradually extinguishing them at the office of Tenebrae we may justly consider with Amalarius as a sign of mourning, or of the sympathy of the church with her divine and suffering Spouse. The precise number of lights is determined by that of the psalms, which is the same as at ordinary matins of three nocturns.

The custom of concealing behind the altar during the last part of the office the last and most elevated candle, and of bringing it forward burning at the end of the service, is a manifest allusion to the death and resurrection of Christ, whose light, as Micrologus observes, is represented by our burning tapers. "I am the light of the world". John VIII. 12[50]. In the same manner the other candles extinguished one after another may represent the prophets successively put to death before their divine Lord: and if we consider that the psalms of the *old Testament* are recited at the time, this explanation may appear more satisfactory than others, which would refer them to the blessed Virgin, the apostles and disciples of Christ[51]. In the triangular form of the candlestick is contained an evident allusion to the B. Trinity. This candlestick is mentioned in a MS. Ordo of the 7th century published by Mabillon.

|*Chant, lamentations.*

The anthems and psalms, with the exception of the *Miserere* which is the last psalm at Lauds, most of the lessons and other parts of the office, are sung in plain chant. From the middle of the 15th century the three lamentations or first three lessons of each day used to be sung in *canto figurato* in the papal chapel: but by order of Sixtus V, only the first lamentation of each day is thus sung, and even it is much shortened, as Clement XII directed: the two others are sung in *canto piano* according to Guidetti's method. The first lamentation both of the first and second day is by the celebrated Pierluigi da Palestrina: that of the third day by Allegri. Baini observes, that the first lamentation of the second day is considered the finest: Palestrina composed it for four voices, besides a bass, which entering at the pathetic apostrophe 'Jerusalem, Jerusalem, be converted to the Lord' "every year makes all the hearers and singers, who have a soul, change colour". Bayni, Mem. Stor. T. 1. The lamentations of Jeremiah have the form of an acrostic, that is, the verses begin with the letters of the Hebrew alphabet in regular order, the first with Aleph, the second with Beth, and so in succession. It was difficult to observe a similar order in the Latin Vulgate: but to preserve some vestige of it, the name of the Hebrew letter, with which each verse begins in the original, is sung before the same verse in the translation.

|*Conclusion of the office.*

When the *Benedictus* or canticle of Zachary and its anthem are finished, the choir sings the verse "Christ was made for us obedient even unto death": on the second night they add "even unto the death of the cross": and on the third, "for which reason God hath exalted him, and hath given him a name, which is above all names". The heart of the christian is melted to devotion by these words, sung on so solemn an occasion: he kneels before his crucified Redeemer, and recites that prayer of love, that prayer of a child to his Father which He that man of sorrows dictated to His beloved disciples; and then remembering those sins, by which he offended that dear and agonising parent, and touched with sorrow and repentance, yet more and more excited by the music, I might almost call it celestial, his heart calls loudly for that mercy to obtain which Jesus died. He joins with God's minister in fervently repeating the prayer imploring God's blessing on those for whom Christ suffered and died: the noise which follows it recals to his mind the confusion of nature at the death of her creator; the lighted candle once more appearing reminds him that His death was only temporary: and he departs in silence impressed with pious sentiments, and inflamed with devout affections.

|Miserere, its music.

They who have assisted at the office of Tenebræ will not be surprised at the saying of a philosopher, that for the advantage of his soul he would wish, that when he was about to render it up to God, he might hear sung the *Miserere* of the Pope's chapel. In no other place has this celebrated music succeeded. Baini the director of the Pontifical choir, in a note to his life of Palestrina, observes that Paride de Grassi, Master of ceremonies to Leo X, mentions that on holy wednesday (A.D. 1519), the singers chanted the *Miserere* in a *new* and *unaccustomed* manner, alternately singing the verses in symphony. This seems to be the origin of the far-famed *Miserere*. Various authors, whom Baini enumerates, afterwards composed *Miserere*[52]; but the celebrated composition of Gregorio Allegri a Roman, who entered the Papal college of singers in 1629, was the most successful, and was for some time sung on all the three days of Tenebræ. Then one composed by Alessandro Scarlatti, or that of Felice Anerio, used to be sung on holy thursday: but these were eclipsed by the *Miserere*, composed in 1214 by Tommase Bai a Bolognese, director of the choir of S. Peter's. From that time only Allegri's and Bai's were sung in the Pope's chapel; till Pius VII directed the celebrated Baini to compose a new *Miserere*, which has received well-merited applause. Since the year 1821 all three, viz. Baini's, Bai's, and Allegri's *Misereres* are sung on the three successive days, and generally in the order in which we have mentioned them: the two latter are sometimes blended together. The first verse is sung in harmony, the second in plain chant, and so successively till the last verse, which alone is sung in harmony by both the choirs, into which the singers are divided; only one choir sings the other verses[53].

On Wednesday-afternoon, the Cardinal great Penitentiary goes in state to S. Mary Major's, where the minor Penitentiaries are Dominicans. For an account of this custom see the preceding chapter. On Wednesday, Thursday and Friday evenings, Christians may be edified at the Trinità dei Pellegrini[54] by the sight of Cardinals, princes, prelates and others, washing in good earnest, and afterwards kissing the feet of poor pilgrims, while they recite with them the Our Father, Hail Mary, Glory be to the Father, and other beautiful prayers, such as;

Gesù, Giuseppe, Maria,

Vi dono il cuore e l' anima mia.

Gesù, Giuseppe, Maria,

Assisteleci nell' ultima agonia, etc.

They afterwards wait on them at table, and accompany them to their beds, reciting other devout prayers. In another part of that establishment, princesses and other ladies practise the same offices of charity towards the female pilgrims. Here might we fancy that the primitive christians were before us, those men of charity, simplicity, and lowliness: and when in the same place, a few years ago, that devout Pontiff Leo XII on his knees washed and kissed the feet of pilgrims, who had journeyed from afar; who that saw him did not call to mind with tears the lowliness and charity of his predecessor Peter, and of a greater than Peter, who "washed the feet of his disciples, and who wiped them with the towel wherewith he was girded".

Marius mourned over the ruins of Carthage; but his was the sorrow of disappointed, selfish ambition. Jeremiah lamented the fall and desolation of Jerusalem: and his plaintive accents were inspired by genuine patriotism and religion. Observe his venerable figure in the Sixtine chapel; there he sits pensive and disconsolate, with his legs crossed, his wearied head resting upon his hand, and his eyes rivetted on the ground, as if nothing could engage his attention but the woes of the daughter of Sion[55]. Then listen to the lamentations of this inspired and afflicted prophet: they are full of deepest pathos, and uttered in notes sweet as the warblings of philomel. Turn now, O Christian soul, to a more sublime and mournful spectacle. Jesus in the garden of Gethsemani and on mount Calvary mourned not for a single city or nation: he sorrowed over the ruins of a world, not as of old Noah may have done, when secure from danger he looked down upon the waters which overspread the earth; but "He was wounded for our iniquities, and he was bruised for our sins: and the Lord hath laid on him the iniquities of us all", He suffered and died for us. The moral ruins of the world, our sins and their awful consequences, caused all the pangs and sorrows of Jesus. Come then let us cast ourselves at the foot of that cross, and cry aloud for mercy with a contrite and humble heart, which He will never despise. To *Thee* alone, shall we say, have we sinned, and have done evil before thee; yet have mercy on us, O God, according to thy great mercy. And thou, O blessed Virgin and Mother, who standest in silent anguish beneath the cross of thy agonising Son[56], would that we could feel love and sorrow like unto thine.

Eja mater fons amoris

Me sentire vim doloris

Fac, ut tecum lugeam.

Fac, ut ardeat cor meum

In amando Christum Deum,

Ut sibi complaceam. Amen.

Footnote 46: (return)

See also Palmer's Origines Liturgicæ, Vol. 1 Antiq. of the English ritual c. 1, p. 1. Both writers do not hesitate to admit that the breviary is the great source of the Church of England's Morning and Evening prayer.

Footnote 47: (return)

Our divine Lord sometimes passed the night in prayer; and the early Christians, as Pliny informs his master Trajan, used to assemble before the light to sing a hymn to Christ. Lucian as well as Ammianus Marcellinus complained of their spending the night in singing hymns. S. Jerome in fine writes to Eustoch. (Ep. 22) that besides the daily hours of prayers we should rise *twice and thrice at night*.

Footnote 48: (return)

In the mass and office for the dead several prayers and ceremonies otherwise prescribed are omitted: so on this occasion, says Benedict XIV, "the church forgetting all things else thinks only of bewailing the sins of mankind, and condoling with Christ our Redeemer in His sufferings". As for the antiquity of this service, Martene remarks (lib. IV, c. 22) that the order of the *nocturnal* and diurnal offices of holy-thursday is found, such as we now observe it, in the ancient Antiphonarium of the Roman church, and in that of S. Gregory published by B. Tommasi, so that there has been scarcely any variation during the last thirteen hundred years.

Footnote 49: (return)

When the Pope officiates, the eight candles over the *cancellata* are lighted: six are lighted for a Cardinal, and four for a Bishop. Amalarius priest of Metz in the ninth century (De ordine antiphonarii), mentions the extinction of the lights in the office of these three days. It would seem however, that it was not then customary at Rome, for Theodore, archdeacon of the Roman church, in answer to his enquiries had said to him "I am usually with the Apostolic Lord at the Lateran, when the office of Coena Domini (Holy Thursday) is celebrated, and it is not customary to extinguish the lights. On Good Friday there is no light of lamps or tapers in the church in Jerusalem (Santa Croce) as long as the Apostolic Lord offers up solemn prayers there, or when the cross is saluted". This latter custom is still continued.

Footnote 50: (return)

In confirmation of this explanation we may observe, that the candle is placed behind the altar after the *Benedictus* during the anthem alluding to Christ's passion, and remains there while the verse 'Christ became obedient unto death' the psalm *Miserere*, and the prayer which mentions the crucifixion, are sung.

Footnote 51: (return)

See such opinions ap. Benedict. XIV, De festis Lib. 1, c. 5. The system of Du Vert, who would reject all mystical and symbolical significations attributed to the church-ceremonies, has been satisfactorily confuted by Langlet, Le Brun, Tournely and other divines.

Footnote 52: (return)

Tartini's and Pisari's lasted only one year each.

Footnote 53: (return)

Persons, who go immediately after the service in the Sixtine chapel to S. Peter's, are generally in time for part if not the whole of the *Miserere* sung in that Basilic. The compositions of Fioravanti the late, Basili the present, master, and Zingarelli, are sung there.

Footnote 54: (return)

See Reminiscences of Rome. Letter 4th. London, 1838 On pilgrimages and pilgrims see Mores Catholici Book 4th, ch. 5th. S. Philip Neri founded the Confraternity of Trinità dei Pellegrini.

Footnote 55: (return)

    ... lia fatto alla guancia

Della sua palma sospirando letto. Dante Pur. VII.

Sed frons læta parum et dejecto lumina vultu. Virg. Æu. VI, 863. See the learned canon. De Jorio's Munica degli antichi, art. Dolore, Mestizia. We may add that conquered provinces are often represented in a similar attitude as statues, on bas-reliefs, and on medals. See for instance, Judæa Capta, a reverse of Vespasian, ap. Addison, Dialogues on ancient medals.

Footnote 56: (return)

"Now there stood by the cross of Jesus his mother". John XIX, 25.

CHAP. IV.

ON THE CEREMONIES OF HOLY THURSDAY

CONTENTS.

General character of the liturgy of holy thursday—its ancient form—blessing of the oils at S. Peter's, communion under one kind—origin and explanation of the blessing and salutation of the oils—High mass in the Sixtine chapel, *troccole*—procession of the B. Sacrament to the Pauline chapel—antiquity of processions—reservation of the B. Sacrament—Papal benediction from S. Peter's, *flabelli*—bull in Coena Domini—washing of the feet—dinner of the *apostles*—antiquity and meaning of this custom of washing feet—customs of other churches: Leonardo da Vinci, Michelangelo, Dante—Cardinals' public dinner etc.—Tenebræ: Card. Penitentiary—recapitulation of the principal ceremonies of the day—S. Peter's on holy thursday-evening: washing of the high-altar—antiquity and meaning of the stripping and washing of the altars—conclusion.

"Before the festival day of the pasch, Jesus knowing that his hour was come, that he should pass out of this world to the Father, having loved his own who were in the world, he loved them to the end". John XIII, 1.

Liturgy of holy-thursday.

During the last three days of holy-week the church celebrates the funeral obsequies of her Divine Spouse: and hence there are numerous signs of mourning in her temples, in her liturgy, and in the dress of her ministers. On thursday however, a passing gleam of heavenly light irradiates the solemn gloom in which she is enveloped: for on this day Jesus Christ, having loved his own even unto the end, instituted the holy sacrament, the staff of our pilgrimage, our solace in affliction, our strength in temptation, the source of all virtue, and the pledge of everlasting life. Accordingly the liturgy of holy-thursday bears the impress both of sorrow and of gladness: it is not unlike a fitful day of April in our northern climes, when the sun now bursts from the clouds which had concealed his brilliancy, and now once more the sky is shrouded in murky gloom—an apt emblem this of the over-changing state of man, who at one moment quaffs the inebriating cup of earthly joys, and yet a little, and it is dashed from his grasp; and sickness, sorrow and death are his portion.

Anciently three masses used to be celebrated at Rome[57] on this day, as is evident from the sacramentary of pope Gelasius; and at all the three the Pope himself officiated. At the first the public penitents were absolved:[58] at the second the oils were blessed; the last (ad vespertinum officium) was intended to commemorate the institution of the blessed Sacrament. Public penance gradually declined in the western church after the seventh century; and the three masses are now reduced to one. That of the Sixtine chapel, at which the Pope assists, differs very little from ordinary Masses celebrated there, and the concourse of persons is generally very great.

Blessing of the oils at S. Peter's

Communion under one kind.

The oils are blessed in S. Peter's during mass, by the Card. archpriest, or a Bishop in his stead. They are three, viz. 1 the oil of catechumens, used in blessing baptism, in consecrating churches and altars, in ordaining priests, and in blessing and crowning sovereigns: 2 the oil of the sick used in administering extreme unction and in blessing bells: 3 sacred chrism, composed of oil, and balm of Gilead or of the west Indies[59]: it is used in conferring baptism and confirmation, in the consecration of bishops, of patens and chalices, and in the blessing of bells. The Roman Pontifical prescribes, that besides the bishop and the usual ministers, there should be present twelve priests, seven deacons, and seven subdeacons, all habited in white vestments. After the elevation at those words of the canon, *Per quem hæc omnia etc.* a little before the *Pater noster*, the Bishop sits down before a table facing the altar, and exorcises and blesses the oil for the sick, which is brought in by a subdeacon. He then proceeds with the mass, and gives communion to the ministers and the rest of the under the form of bread alone[60]. Having received the ablutions, he returns to the table above mentioned, and awaits the coming of the procession of the priests, deacons, subdeacons etc. In it, the balsam is carried by a subdeacon, etc. the oil for the chrism and that for the catechumens by two deacons: and meantime the choir sings appropriate verses. The bishop blesses the balsam, and mixes it with some oil; he then breathes three times in the form of a cross over the vessel of chrism, as do the twelve priests also. Next follows the blessing, and then the salutation, of the chrism: the latter is made 3 times by the bishop and each of the twelve priests in succession, saying, Hail holy chrism, after which they kiss the vessel which contains it. The oil of catechumens is blessed and saluted in like manner: and the procession returns to the sacristy; in the mean time the bishop concludes the mass; and thus this solemn rite terminates.

Origin of the blessing of the oils.

The oil of the sick is mentioned in the well-known passage of St. James V, 14 "Is any man sick among you; let him bring in the priests of the church, and let them pray over him, anointing him with oil in the name of the Lord etc." At the beginning of the fifth century also, Pope Innocent I observes that it is the office of the bishop to make or prepare (*conficere*) this "holy of chrism" or unction: and in the Sacramentary of Pope Gregory the great the rite; by which this oil was blessed and administered to the sick, is described. Chrism and the oil of catechumens also are mentioned by many ancient Fathers. (See Turnely T. 7 de Sacram. Bapt. et Confirm, etc.)[61] St. Basil in the 4th century attributes the origin of the custom of blessing the oils to tradition. "We bless the water of baptism and the *oil of unction*, as well as the person who receives baptism. By what scriptures? Is it not from silent and secret tradition?" (De Spir. S. c. 27). It is mentioned also in the second and third councils of Carthage, by S. Cyprian, who says "The eucharist, and the oil, with which the baptised are anointed, are sanctified at the altar". Ep. 70.

It would appear however from the 20th canon of the first council of Toledo that anciently chrism could be blessed *at any time*; and hence Benedict XIV is of opinion, that the custom of blessing it only on holy Thursday began about the seventh century; for it is mentioned in the Sacramentary of S. Gregory, in the old Ordo Romanus, and in other works written after that period. This day has been with reason chosen for this ceremony, as St. Thomas observes, in order that the chrism may be prepared for the solemn baptism administered on Easter Eve; and because on it the Eucharistic sacrament, for which the other sacraments are as it were preparatory, was instituted. S. Isidore however assigns a different reason, viz. that two days before the pasch Mary *anointed* the head and feet of the Lord". De Divi Off. lib. 2, c. 28.

Meaning of the ceremonies already described.

Pouget (Institut. Cath. t. 2, c. 8) proves that the blessing of the oils originates in apostolic tradition, as St. Basil cited above observes. He proves also that since the fifth and sixth centuries the bishop and priests used to breathe three times over the chrism and oil of catechumens, and to salute them with the words "Ave sanctum chrisma: ave sanctum oleum". Our Saviour breathed on His apostles, when He said 'Receive ye the holy Ghost': and hence his ministers breathe over the chrism, by which the Holy Ghost is conferred in confirmation, and over the oil of catechumens, which is used in other sacred rites. Respect is paid to them, because they are employed in God's service, and hence it is a relative respect directed to Him. An ardent soul will never hesitate to address inanimate objects; in fact some of the finest passages of ancient and modern oratory are apostrophes of this nature[62]. S. Andrew is said to have saluted the cross, on which he suffered, S. Paula the birth-place of our divine Lord; and theirs were words of love of God, and not of idolatry.

In the Sixtine chapel the crucifix and tapestry over the altar are covered with a white and not a purple veil; the throne also is white, and the Pope is vested in a white cope. On the rich facing of the altar is represented Christ dead, His descent into limbo, and His resurrection. The cardinal dean generally celebrates the high mass, after the *Gloria in excelsis* of which no bells are allowed to be tolled in Rome (except at the papal benediction) but in their stead are used *troccole* or boards struck with iron: this practice is observed until the *Gloria in excelsis* is sung in the papal chapel on the following saturday-morning[63].

After the offertory of the mass Palestrina's motet *Fratres ego enim* is sung; of which Baini says that he "does not hesitate to affirm that it resembles as closely as possible the music of heaven". Two hosts are consecrated, one of which is received by the celebrant, and the other destined for the following day is put into a chalice, which the deacon covers with a paten and *palla* or linen cloth, as the dead body of Christ was wrapped in "fine linen"[64]. Mark XV, 46. At the beginning of the canon twelve lighted torches are brought in by *bussolanti*; and after the elevation two masters of ceremonies distribute among the cardinals and others candles carried by clerks of the chapel, in preparation for the procession. The usual kiss of peace is not given, from detestation of the treacherous kiss given this day by Judas to his divine master, as Alcuin remarks[65].

Immediately after mass the cardinal celebrant with his ministers leaves the chapel; the other cardinals, bishops and mitred abbots, put on their respective sacred vestments, and the *Uditori di Rota*, the *Cherici di Camera, Votanti,* and *Abbreviatiori*, their surplices: the other prelates wear their usual *cappe*. They all now accompany the B. Sacrament to the Pauline chapel[66] in solemn procession, which is regulated like that of palm-Sunday. The singers go to the *sala regia*, illuminated with large cornucopia, and there begin to sing the *Pange lingua* (a hymn in honour of the holy Sacrament) as soon as the cross covered with a purple veil appears: the last verses of it are sung in the Pauline chapel, which is splendidly illuminated. The cardinals bearing their mitres and torches precede two by two the Holy Father, who bare-headed and on foot carries the blessed Sacrament under a canopy supported by eight assistant bishops or protonotaries[67]. When the Pope reaches the altar, the first cardinal deacon receives from His hands the B. Sacrament, and preceded by torches carries it to the upper part of the *macchina*; M. Sagrista places it within the urn commonly called the sepulchre, where it is incensed by the Pope; in the mean time the conclusion of the hymn is sung. M. Sagrista then shuts the sepulchre, and delivers the key to thy Card. Penitentiary, who is to officiate on the following day.

|Reservation of the B. Sacrament.

Two objects are obtained by this custom; 1st. the blessed sacrament is solemnly preserved for the adoration of the faithful on this anniversary of its institution, as well as for the priest's communion on good friday[68]; 2nd. the burial of our divine Saviour is represented: this is anticipated, in order that the principal altar may be striped, in sign of mourning, and as He was stripped before His crucifixion.

|Papal benediction: flabelli.

|Bulla in Coena Domina.

The procession, of which we have already spoken, afterwards proceeds from the Pauline chapel to the *loggia* in front of S. Peter's: but the Pope, as he no longer carries the B. Sacrament, wears his mitre, and is seated in his *sedia gestatoria* under a canopy carried by eight Referendarii[69]; and the *flabelli*[70] are carried at each side of Him. He now gives his solemn benediction to the multitude assembled before St. Peter's. This however is repeated with even greater splendour on Easter-Sunday, as well as on the Ascension and Assumption; and we shall therefore reserve a description of it to another occasion, especially since generally speaking, persons who are anxious to witness the *lavanda* or washing of the feet will find it difficult to be present also at the Benediction[71].

|Washing of the feet.

After the benediction, the cardinals and others take off their sacred vestments, and resume their *cappe*, which they wear during the *lavanda* or washing of the feet. This now takes place in S. Peters, in a side-chapel adorned with two *arazzi*; one representing Leonardo Da Vinci's last supper is placed behind the benches prepared for the priests whose feet are to be washed by the Pope: and the other, which represents Providence seated on the globe between Justice and Charity, above two lions holding banners of the church, is placed over the throne. The Pope is habited in a red cope, and wears a mitre. Seated on His throne, and surrounded by cardinals, prelates, and other dignitaries of His court, He puts incense into the thurible, being assisted as usual by the first Cardinal priest. He then gives the blessing, usual before the gospel is sung, to the Cardinal-deacon habited in his sacred vestments, who sings that beautiful passage of the gospel of S. John, which explains the origin of this ceremony: "Jesus knowing that his hour was come, that he should pass out of this world to the Father, having loved his own who were in the world, he loved them to the end. Knowing that the Father had given him all things into his hands, he began to wash the feet of his disciples, and wipe them with the towel wherewith he was girded, and he said to them; If I being Lord and Master have washed your feet, you also ought to wash one another's feet; for I have given you an example, that as I have done to you, so you do also". At the end of the gospel, the Pope kisses the book, the Cardinal Deacon incenses Him as usual, and the choir begins to sing beautiful anthems allusive to the affecting ceremony, and recommending charity, the distinctive virtue of Christians, more precious than even faith and hope. The Pope's cope is then taken off, and a towel is fastened to his girdle by the assisting Card. deacons; and then, in imitation of his Divine Master, he washes and kisses the right foot[72] of 13 priests, called the *apostles*, dressed in *cappe* of white cloth, and wearing high cap, which in form resemble those on the bas-reliefs of Persepolis: each of them receives from Him a towel, and a nosegay, besides a gold and silver medal presented by the Treasurer[73]. The Pope then returns to his throne, washes his hands[74] is vested once more in the cope, and recites the Our Father and the concluding prayers.

|Dinner of the apostles.

His Holiness afterwards waits on the 13 *apostles* at table, in a hall in the Vatican palace, (at present in the hall above the portico of S. Peter's), giving them water to wash their hands, helping them to soup, one or more dishes, and pouring out wine and water for them once or twice. The plates are handed to Him by prelates of *mantelletta*, and during the ceremony one of His chaplains reads a spiritual book. He then gives them his blessing, washes His hands, and departs. "Which is greater" says our Saviour, "he that sitteth at table or he that serveth? Is not he that sitteth at table? but I am in the midst of you as he that serveth?"

|Antiquity and meaning of the lavanda.

From the most remote antiquity, it was customary among the Hebrews and other nations, that the feet of strangers and guests should be washed before they reclined at table, as they had often travelled on foot. Thus the angels entertained by Abraham and Lot (Gen. XVIII, XIX), were supplied with water to wash their feet: Abraham's servants in the house of Laban, and the brothers of Joseph, when received by him, washed their feet. (Gen. XLIII, 24)[75]. In these cases however the guest washed his own feet; and hence the condescension of our Divine Lord was an act not of hospitality or charity alone, but also of profound humility; and accordingly he put on a towel or apron, like an ordinary slave, as Ferrari observes (De Re Vestiaria par. 1). Most interpreters are of opinion, that Christ washed the feet of His disciples towards the close of the ordinary supper, and shortly before He instituted the holy Sacrament; in order to signify the purity with which it should be received. His example was imitated by His disciples, and accordingly S. Paul

(1 Tim. V, 10) speaks of widows who "have washed the saints' feet," as Magdalen had washed those of our Lord.

In the Roman church, as in that of Bologna, it has been for many ages customary for the Bishop to wash feet on this day. In the *Ordo Romanus* of Cencius Camerarius it is mentioned, that the Roman Pontiff after mass washed the feet of twelve subdeacons, and after dinner of 13 poor persons, or according to the Ordines Romani published by Mabillon, of 12 deacons. The *Ceremoniale*, attributed to Marcellus archbishop of Corcyra, prescribes that the Pope should wash the feet of thirteen poor men. Various causes are assigned by different authors to explain, why the number is thirteen, and not twelve as was that of the apostles. (See Benedict XIV, De Festis, lib. I, c. VI, §§ 57, 58). The most probable account, we think, is that the thirteenth *apostle* was added in memory of the angel, who is believed to have appeared among the 12 poor guests of S. Gregory the great, while he was exercising united charity and humility. A painting of this event may be seen in one of the chapels near his church on the Cælian mount, in which is preserved the table, at which he daily fed twelve poor persons. (See the passage of John the deacon cited above in the note). The two customs of washing the feet first of 12, and then of 13, have been reduced to one, and in it the number 13 is preserved[76].

|*Cardinals' public dinner.*

Till within the last few years the Cardinals used to dine in public at the Vatican on holy Thursday and good Friday, that they might be spared the trouble of returning to their respective palaces before Tenebræ; and anciently the Pope used to dine with them at the Lateran palace, in the hall called the Triclinium Leonianum[77]. The Pontiff wore on such occasions his cope and mitre, and the Cardinals were habited in sacred vestments with mitres. After dinner a sermon was preached before the Cardinals. *Mons. Maggiordomo* used to invite on these days prelates, officers, and others engaged in the *cappella* or palace, to a dinner at which he presided.

|*Tenebræ etc.*

In the afternoon, at the office of Tenebræ, among other signs of mourning, the cross is veiled in black, and the candles are of yellow wax: the Pope's throne is stripped of its usual ornaments, and is without a canopy: the cardinals' and prelates' benches also are without carpets. The Cardinal Penitentiary goes to S. Peter's, where the minor Penitentiaries are Conventuals of S. Francis. We have spoken on these subjects in the preceding chapters. We may here recapitulate the principal ceremonies of the day, as Morcelli has done in his Calendar. The oils are blessed in S. Peter's; the Pope assists at mass in the Sixtine chapel, carries the B. Sacrament to the Pauline chapel, gives His solemn benediction from S. Peter's, washes the feet of thirteen priests and serves them at table. In the afternoon Tenebrae in the Sixtine chapel; and the Cardinal great Penitentiary goes to S Peter's.

S. Peter's on holy thursday-evening.

In this basilic the B. Sacrament is preserved amid many lights in the *Sepulchre* in a side-chapel[78], and several confraternities come in procession to venerate the relics, of which we shall speak in the next chapter. It is much to be regretted that the cross, which used on holy-Thursday and good-Friday to glow with 628 lights[79], and to produce a splendid effect by the *chiaroscuro* which resulted from it in this vast and magnificent fabric, is no longer suspended before the Confession, in consequence of irreverent conduct on preceding occasions.

Washing of the altar.

There still remains another remarkable ceremony customary in S. Peter's on holy-Thursday. After the office of Tenebræ, the chapter of that basilica proceeds in procession from the chapel of the choir to the high altar. The black stoles which six of the canons wear, and the yellow and extinguished tapers of the acolythes, are signs of mourning for the sufferings of Christ. They all carry elegant *aspergilli*[80] of box or other wood, and having prayed for a short time in silence, they chant the anthem "They divided my garments etc." and the psalm "O God, my God, why hast thou abandoned me?" A fine cloth, which covered the altar, is then removed from it, and the Cardinal-priest of the church and the six canons pour whine upon the altar, and wash it with their *aspergilli* or brushes. After the other canons, beneficed clergymen, etc. have in turn washed it in like manner: the Cardinal and the six canons begin to dry it with sponges and towels: all then kneel down, and the ceremony concludes with the verse "Christ became obedient unto death etc." the Our Father, and the prayer of the day "Look down, we beseech thee etc."[81] The chapter then venerates the relics shewn as usual from the gallery above S. Veronica's statue.

45

The *stripping* of the altars, which is practised on this day throughout the western church, is mentioned in the most ancient *Ordo Romanus*: indeed anciently the altars used to be stripped every day, as Du Vert (Ceremon. de l'Eglise T. IV.) and Cancellieri (De Secretariis T. IV.) have shewn. The custom of *washing* the altar is observed in the Latin church in those of the Dominicans and Carmelites; and also according to Benedict XIV "in many churches of France, Germany and other remote countries" among which Cancellieri reckons Spain. It is mentioned by S. Isidore (lib. de Eccles. Offic. c. 18) by Alcuin (de divinis offic.) and in the Sarum, Parisian and many other missals quoted by Martene. What however is its meaning? While Monsignor Battelli, in his dissertation on the subject, maintains that this custom was instituted for the sake of cleanliness, rather than from a wish to denote any mystery, and that this day was selected as the most convenient, because the altars were already stripped; the abbot Rupert and Belet discover mystical meanings in the sponges, towels, wine, water, and even *aspergilli*. We prefer a middle course, and while we are willing to admit with Durandus and others an allusion in the wine and water to the blood and water which flowed from our Saviour on the cross, we maintain with the learned S. Isidore, S. Eligius, Benedict XIV and others, that we wash the altar, the symbol of Christ, from motives of respect to Him, who on this day washed the feet of His disciples.

Two great virtues are embodied in the ceremonies of this day, and impart to them their life and loveliness: they are the essential and characteristic virtues of Christians, by the practice of which they imitate their divine Master and model, and come at last to be united to Him in heaven. Christ was moved by charity to institute the Holy Sacrament, and by humility to wash His disciples feet. Let us then learn of him because He was meek and humble of heart, and let us love one another, because Christ hath first loved us, and commands us to love one another.

Footnote 57: (return)

In Africa two were customary, one in the morning, and the other after supper. S. August. ep. 54 ad Januarium.

Footnote 58: (return)

For an account of this ancient ceremony the reader may see Fleury, Moeurs des Chretiens; *Funz. della Settimana Santa.* Martene, lib. IV, 22. etc.

Footnote 59: (return)

"Balsam is produced in the vineyards of Engaddi, and in preparing chrism it is mixed with oil and consecrated by the pontifical benediction, that all the faithful may be signed with this unction at confirmation". Ven. Bede, in canlic. cap. I. The Greeks bless the chrism on the same day as the Latins, having prepared it a few days previously. See their Euchelogium, Ordo VIII entitled, On the composition of the great ointment in the Costantinop. church ap. Martene, loc. cit.

Footnote 60: (return)

Only one priest says mass in each on this day and the other priests communicate, as on it Christ alone said mass, and distributed the Holy communion to the apostles. Although for many centuries both kinds were ordinarily received, yet the custom of communicating under the form of bread alone is very ancient. Thus in time of persecution the faithful used to carry to their houses the holy communion under the form of bread alone, the hermits also preserved it in the deserts, the sick received it as their viaticum, the ministers of God kept it in the churches, for their spiritual support, and the bishops used to send it to their clergy in token of their union in charity. These were all instances of communion under one kind, which are enumerated and proved by many Catholic divines, as for instance by Dr. Rock in his Hierurgia. They demonstrate the constant belief of the church, that the whole sacrament is received under one kind only; and Christ himself in the scriptures attributes its admirable effects to the act of *eating* only as well as to that of *eating and drinking*. "He that eateth this bread shall live for ever" etc. In fact since His resurrection "He dieth now no more": His body and blood and soul and Divinity are united together for evermore, and consequently the communicant receives under the form of bread alone Christ himself whole and entire. The Latin church prescribed the general reception of communion under one kind, in order to obviate accidents which frequently arose from the indiscriminate use of the chalice, and in opposition to the error of the Hussites: Thus Paul II took occasion from the presence of Frederic III at Rome, to give a public and illustrious proof of the condemnation of this new heresy by the church, by giving communion under one kind only to the Emperor, and also to the deacon and subdeacon, who generally communicate under both kinds when the Pope sings mass. In the Greek and other oriental churches communion is administered under one kind to the sick and others who are prevented by distance from communicating in the churches. The general communion customary on holy-thursday is prescribed by the English bishop Walter in the 10th century, in the capitulary of Theodulph of Orleans, and by all ancient pontificals and missals, according to Martene T. 3, p. 98. It is practised also by the Greeks, as Leo Allatius testifies. De consensu utriusque Ecclesiæ lib. 3. Palmer (Vol. 2. p. 76) says "It is not essential to the validity of the Sacrament, that the bread should be whole and entire before consecration, and broken afterwards: but the Universal practice of the Christian church, derived from the apostles and from Jesus Christ himself ought not to be infringed in this matter". Yet even Bp. Middleton whom he quotes in the same page, says "When there were many communicants, *in primitive times, there were several cakes or loaves*, in proportion to the number: and it took some time after the consecration was finished, to break and divide them for distribution". Each person communicated from his own offering: hence S. Augustine says "Erubescere debet homo idoneus si de aliena oblatione communicaverit" Serm. 215 de Temp, any longer justification of the general practice of the Roman church would therefore be superfluous.

Footnote 61: (return)

"From the frequent mention of *oil* in scripture as the emblem of spiritual gifts it was actually used in the primitive church in the ceremonies of admitting catechumens, and in baptising". Tracts of the Times, Vol. 1, no. 34.

Footnote 62: (return)

Our ardent love of this classic soil tempts us to insert the following noble instance from Cicero (pro Milone XXXI) "Vos enim jam *Albani* tumuli atque luci vos, inquam, imploro alque tester vosque Albanorum obrutæ aræ, sacrorum populi Romani sociæ et æquales, quas ille præceps amentia cæsis prostratisque sanctissimi lucis substructionum insanis molibus oppresserat: vestræ tum aræ, vestræ religiones viguerunt, vestra vis valuit, quam ille (Clodius) omni scelere polluarat: tuque ex tuo edito monte, Latiaris sancte Jupiter, cujus ille lacus, nemora, finesque

47

sæpe omni nefario stupro et scelere macularat, aliquaudo ad eum puniendum oculos aperuisti: vobis illæ, vobis vestro in conspecta seræ sed justæ tamen et debitæ pænæ solutæ sunt".

Footnote 63: (return)

These *troccole* were formerly called by the hard names of *crepitacula ligna congregantia, mallei excitatorii*. The Greeks used them anciently, as Martene proves from a libellus de miraculis Anastasii presented to the second council of Nice, from S. John Chrysostom's life by Metaphrastes etc. etc. In modern times also they continue to use them. Benedict XIV observes that the practice of the Latin church on these days is intended to preserve the remembrance of the ancient custom. It is also evidently intended, like the reversed arms of the soldiers, as a sign of mourning for the death of Christ. This silence of the bells is prescribed in the ancient rituals: mystical interpreters assign as a reason, that they signify Christ's preachers and apostles, who were silent during the sufferings of their Master.

Footnote 64: (return)

S. Greg. Turon. De mirac. S. Martini "oblatis super altare sacris muneribus, mysterioque Corporis et Sanguinis Christi palla ex more cooperto.", Vid. Bona. Lib. II, c. 13. not. 12.

Footnote 65: (return)

This mass is found in the Antiphonary and Sacramentary of Pope Gregory the great; in all churches but the Roman, as Marlene observes, vespers were joined with the mass on this day, as they are on holy Saturday throughout the Latin church. On holy-thursday the Pope used generally to preach after the gospel, and in the mean time the Cardinals stripped the altar: after the sermon the Pope blessed the people as usual, and then began the *Credo*, according to Benedict, Canon of S. Peter's. His Holiness drank on this day directly from the chalice, and did not use the golden reed or *fistola*, as on other occasions; this we learn from the Apamean Pontifical.

Footnote 66: (return)

This chapel was erected by Paul III according to the design of Antonio Sangallo. Its two large frescoes are the last efforts of the genius of Michelangelo, then aged 75 years: they represent the crucifixion of S. Peter and the conversion of S. Paul. The fall of Simon Magus, and the baptism conferred by S. Peter, painted on the righthand-wall are works of Federico Zuccheri; on the opposite side S. Paul at Malta, and restoring the young man, who had fallen from a window, are by Lorenzo Sabbatino da Bologna, the ceiling was painted by Federico Zuccheri. The B. Sacrament is publicly and solemnly exposed in this chapel for the adoration of the faithful on the first Sunday of Advent as well as on holy-thursday See Chaltard; *Descriz. del Vaticano* Taja, *Palazzo Vaticano*.

Footnote 67: (return)

S. John Chrysostom established processions at Constantinople in opposition to those of the Arians; and the empress Eudoxia supplied the people with silver crosses and wax lights, to be carried on such occasions. Socrat. Hist. Eccl. lib. VI, c. 8, Sozomen lib. VIII, c. 8. Processions were incompatible with the persecutions of the first three centuries. During them, and even long after Constantine, in consequence of the discipline of secrecy, there was neither public exposition or procession of the B. Sacrament. The faithful however adored it privately, as for instance, S. Gregory Nazianzen relates of his sister Gorgonia, that when seized by a fever "she fell down with faith before the altar, and invoked with a loud cry Him who is honoured thereupon". (Discourse on her funeral). S. Cyril of Jerusalem also exhorts the believer, that when he receives the chalice of the blood of Christ he should bow down profoundly and adore. (Catech. 5), The office and mass of Corpus Christi were composed by S. Thomas Aquinas. As holy-thursday is in great part devoted to the sufferings of Christ, the festival of *Corpus Christi* with its procession was instituted about the middle of the thirteenth century by Urban IV at the petition of B. Juliana of Mount *Cornelione*, and in consequence of the miracle of Bolsena, well known as the subject of one of Raffaello's frescoes in the Vatican. See Bened. XIV, De Festis, and the authors cited by him. The miraculous corporal stained with blood is still preserved at Orvieto, the celebrated cathedral of which owes its foundation to the miracle. "No one eats that flesh, says S. Augustine, unless he has first adored" in ps. 98 "The flesh of Christ," says S. Ambrose "which we adore even now in the mysteries, and which the apostles adored in the Lord Jesus" (de Spir. S. lib. 34, c. 12) All the fathers and liturgies mention this adoration, which was therefore derived from apostolic tradition. Sala ad Bonæ lib. 2, c. 13.

Footnote 68: (return)

In the Greek church communion is on this day reserved for the sick of the ensuing year under the form of bread alone, according to Leo Allatius. (De utriusque Ecclesiæ consensione). Pope Innocent I in the beginning of the 5th century directs, that the eucharist be preserved on this day for the priest and the sick. This reservation is mentioned also in the Gregorian sacramentary, without any mention of the sacred blood, since it might be spilt. It has taken place in the Pauline chapel ever since its erection by Paul III. A particle of the B. Sacrament was formerly preserved after mass on festivals and carried back in procession to the sacristy: it was carried to the altar in procession on the next festival, and a portion or the whole of it was put into the chalice before the host was broken. See Cancellieri, De Secretariis T. I, p. 217, seq.

Footnote 69: (return)

These prelates used to refer cases and petitions to the Popes, as they now do the former to their tribunal, which according to Gonzalez derives its name of *Segnatura* from the *signature* of the sovereign affixed to its decree.

Footnote 70: (return)

They are formed of peacocks' feathers, the eyes of which according to Macri and others signify the vigilance and circumspection of the Pontiffs. They are mentioned in the apostolic constitutions, in which it is prescribed, that two deacons should hold, them in order to drive away flies, which might otherwise fall into the chalice. Accordingly, at the ordination of the deacons in the Greek church, among other instruments a Flabellum is given to them for their ministry at the altar: this S. Anastasius is said to have used while a deacon. Flabella are mentioned in the liturgies of SS. Basil, Chrisostom, and other Greek and Syriac liturgies, Flabella are in the Latin church a mark of distinction, and are carried for the Grand Prior of the knights of Malta the bishop of Troja in Aquila, and the archbishop of Messina, as well as for His Holiness.

Footnote 71: (return)

Since the time of Clement XIV, the custom of reading from the *loggia* on this day the bull in *Coena Domini* has been abolished. (On this bull see de Maistre du Pape lib. 2, c. 14). According to the doctrine of S. Paul, the B. Sacrament is the bond as it is the symbol of union or *communion* between the faithful; "We being many are one body, all who partake of one bread" 1 Cor. X, 17, and hence this day of its institution was selected for the public *excommunication* of those, who reject the doctrines of the church, or maliciously oppose her ordinances. After the bull had been read "many candles are lighted, of which the Lord Pope himself holds some, and each cardinal and prelate one lighted, and he extinguishes and throws them on the ground, saying, we excommunicate all the aforesaid; and then the bells are rung together without observing any order". Ap. Gatticuin, Acta Cerem. 82. These ceremonies are interpreted to mean the *extinction of the grace* of the holy Ghost; and the dispersion of unbelievers, as on the contrary the regular and orderly ringing of bells calls the faithful together.

Footnote 72: (return)

It is supported by the subdeacon habited in the tunic or *tonacella*.

Footnote 73: (return)

John the deacon, in his life of Gregory the great, mentions the *Sacellarius* or Treasurer (see Thomassin lib. 2. c. 103, n. 11), whom that holy Pope commanded according to custom to invite the twelve pilgrims to dinner. Besides the gifts mentioned above, the white dress is given to these *apostles*, who are chosen by some Cardinals, Ambassadors, the Propaganda, the *Maggiordomo*, and the captain of the Swiss guards.

Footnote 74: (return)

The water is brought to him by the Prince assisting at the throne, and the towel is presented by the first Cardinal Priest. When the Pope is prevented from performing this ceremony, the Cardinal Dean supplies his place in presence of the sacred college (Lunadoro). In that case the gospel is sung, not by a cardinal, but by the prelate who is deacon of the *cappella*. Formerly, according to the MS. Pontifical of the Apamean church written in 1214, Vespers were sung by the Pope's chaplains, while he washed the feet of twelve subdeacons.

Footnote 75: (return)

Chardin and other travellers testify, that this practice is preserved in modern times. In Homer's Odyssey the custom of taking a bath before a banquet is frequently mentioned, III, 467; IV, 49, VI. 216; VIII, 449.

Footnote 76: (return)

The emperors of Costantinople used (according to Codinus De Officiis Aulæ Costantinop.) to wash the feet of twelve poor persons: and Vespasiano Fiorentino in the fifteenth century, in his life of Alfonso di Napoli quoted by Cancellieri, says that "Il Giovedi Santo lavava i piedi a tanti poveri, quant' egli aveva anni, et lavavagli, come si deve ... et a tutti dava una veste bianca, et un pajo di calze, et un Alfonsino, et un fiorino et un carlino, et non so che altra moneta. Dipoi il Giovedi medesímo faceva ordinare una cena,... et la Maestà del Re la pigliava, et metteva loro innanzi, e con il vino, et quello avevano di bisogno con grandissima umiltà". See also Martene, De Ant. Eccl. Rit. Lib. IV, c. XII, § 8. Our readers will here call to mind the good old custom still preserved of the maundy of our British Sovereigns, so called from mandatum, the first word of the first anthem sung during, the washing of the feet. In the Greek church, according to Baillet, not only are the feet of twelve poor persons washed, but the name of an apostle is given to each of them; as it may be supposed, nobody is anxious to have the name of Judas Iscariot: so lots are drawn to determine the person who is to represent that traitor. This may remind us of the threat of Leonardo da Vinci to copy the head of Judas, in his celebrated last supper, from the importunate Prior of S. Maria delle Grazie of Milan. Poor Leonardo despaired of finding a model for the head of our Saviour; and for more than a year was seeking the rabble for a fit subject whom he might represent as Judas: meantime the Prior was continually worrying him to finish the fresco. "In ogni caso poi" said he to Lodovico Sforza, "faro capitale del ritratto del P. Priore, che lo merita per la sua importunità e per la sua poca discrezione". The story of Leonardo bears some resemblance to the manner in which Michelangelo punished Biagio da Cesena Pontifical Master of Ceremonies, who before Daniel of Volterra had acquired his well-known nickname of *braghettone* complained to the Pope, that the naked figures of the last judgment were unworthy of a house of prayer. The artist introduced his censor in his painting as Minos judge of the infernal regions, with long ears like those of the other devils, and a serpent's tail. Paul III when appealed to is said to have answered, that if his Ceremoniere had been in Purgatory, he might have helped him out, but out of hell there was no redemption. This Papal witticism Platner could not find in any writer earlier than Richardson (See Beschreibung der Stadt Rom) but *se non è vero, è ben trovato*. Dante was not more scrupulous than Michelangelo about thrusting his opponents into his *inferno*.

Pictoribus atque poetis

Quidlibet audendi semper fuit æqua potestas.

Footnote 77: (return)

The mosaics with which it was adorned by Pope Leo III are preserved in the great niche adjoining the *scala santa*.

Footnote 78: (return)

The Portuguese, Spanish and some other churches are generally distinguished on this day by the brilliancy of the illumination of their *sepulchres*.

Footnote 79: (return)

In the eighth century Pope Hadrian I, according to Anastasius, suspended under the principal or *triumphal* arch, as it was called, a silver cross with 1365 or 1380 small lamps, which where lighted at Easter and other great festivals. This was perhaps the origin of the cross which used to be suspended in S. Peter's at this season.

Footnote 80: (return)

We have already mentioned an ancient Christian fresco in which an aspergillum is represented.

Footnote 81: (return)

Formerly, as Card. Borgia has proved (De Cruce Vaticana) this ceremony was performed in S. Peter's on good Friday. In other churches there were two distinct observances; 1. that of stripping the altars on holy Thursday, when Christ's passion began; and 2. that of washing them with wine and on good Friday, when blood and water flowed from His side, as the Abbot Rupert observes. For the ancient ceremonies of this day at Rome see besides the Apamean Pontifical above-cited, the Pontificals of Egebert archbishop of York and of Tirpin archbishop of Rheims ap. Martene, loc. cit. In some places the fast of Lent was not observed on this day, as appears from S. Augustine, Ep. 54 and Januarium. Of old this was the day for shaving in preparation for Easter-Sunday: it was therefore called shere-Thursday.

CHAP. V.

ON THE CEREMONIES OF GOOD-FRIDAY

CONTENTS.

Ancient ceremonies at Rome—Service in the Sixtine chapel—Passio—Sermon and indulgence—Prayers for all mankind—exposition of the cross; ancient crucifixes and crosses—*adoration* of the cross; its antiquity—Palestrina's *improperii*, Trisagion—chant of the hymn *Pange lingua gloriosi lauream etc*,—Procession of the B. Sacrament—*Mass* of the Presanctified, Vespers—Tenebræ—Veneration of the principal relics at S Peter's—Grounds of belief in the genuineness of relics—1. Relic of the cross—2. of the lance—3. *Volto Santo*—Reflections—Recapitulation.

"*The principal object of the church in the office of this day is, that Jesus Christ crucified may be placed before our eyes, that touched with contrition at the sight, our souls may be so disposed, as to obtain the fruit of redemption*" Bened. XIV, De Festis D.N.J.C. lib. 1. c. 7.

|*Ancient ceremonies.*

On good Friday the Pope used formerly to go with the Cardinals and the other members of the court to the Oratory of S. Lorenzo called *Sancta Sanctorum* in the Lateran palace, where they venerated and kissed the relics of SS. Peter and Paul, as well as two crosses preserved there. One of these was then carried by a Cardinal Priest, and and the Host consecrated on the preceding day was borne by another Cardinal of the same order; the Pope, the Cardinals and all the others were bare-footed, and walked in procession reciting psalms to S. John Lateran's and thence to S. Croce, where the station was held and the ceremonies of the day were performed.[82]

|*Service in the Sixtine chapel.*

|*Passio.*

|*Sermon and indulgence.*

These take place at present in the Sixtine chapel; in which the yellow colour of the candles and torches, the nakedness of the Pope's throne and of the seats of the church denote the desolation of the church at the sufferings and death of her divine founder. The Cardinals do not wear their rings; their dress is of purple, which is their mourning colour; in like manner the Bishops do not wear rings and their stockings are black: those of the Cardinals are purple; and the maces as well as the soldiers' arms are reversed. The Card. great Penitentiary with the sacred ministers are habited in black. There is no thurifer and there are no lights; for the death of the Son of God is going to be commemorated; and while He was hanging upon the cross and when He died, there was darkness over the whole earth. The Pope is habited in a red cope: he does not wear his ring nor give his blessing: but if he be present at this part of the service, His Holiness kneeling with the Card. Penitentiary at his left hand offers up prayers for a short time before the altar. This, which was stripped on the preceding day, is now covered with a linen cloth by two *Cerimonieri*[83]. The Pope then goes to His seat; and the Card. Celebrant accompanied by the ministers to the altar, and thence to his *faldistorio* or seat. An appropriate passage from the prophecy of Osee is sung by one of the choir, and the precept from Exodus concerning the killing of the paschal-lamb, a type of Christ, by the subdeacon. The Pope and the Card. Celebrant also read both these lessons, after each of which a tract is sung by the choir; and between them a prayer by the Celebrant. After the prophecies, which are a powerful confirmation of the truth of our holy religion, the account of the sufferings and death of Jesus Christ, penned by an eye-witness S. John, the disciple of love, is recited[84]. It is read in a low voice by the Card. Celebrant and sung with the same impressive chant as on Palm-Sunday by three cantors wearing the alb, a black maniple and stole: they used formerly to recite it bare-footed. At those words "And bowing down his head he gave up the ghost" all kneel to adore their Redeemer. It is related of a servant of God of the name of Piccolomini, that he expired in church on good Friday when those words were sung. The latter part is chanted, but without the usual ceremonies, by the deacon, after he has taken off his folded chasuble and put on the large band or stole. A short sermon is then preached by a conventual Friar, who afterwards according to custom publishes the indulgence or remission of temporal punishment of thirty years granted by the Pope to those who have confessed and sincerely repented of their sins. See p. 37. As Morinus has shewn (De Penitentia cap. 4.) in most churches penitents were absolved and reconciled after the gospel.

|Prayers for all mankind.

Christ, says S. Paul, died for all men, and when suffering on the cross, He prayed even for his relentless persecutors: on the anniversary then of his death it is fit that His church should pray for all men, that all may be saved by the application of His merits to their souls. The Card. Celebrant commences the beautiful, charitable, and ancient prayers of this day with the words, Let us pray, dearly beloved, for the holy church of God etc. The deacon then kneeling says (according to the ancient custom mentioned by S. Cesarius of

Arles in his 36th homily, and by S. Basil in his book on the Holy Ghost c. XXVII) Let us bend our knees, and the subdeacon answers, Stand up, as it was customary to pray standing. This form is repeated before each prayer, except that which is offered for the Jews[85]: for their soldiers, bowing the knee before our Lord, mocked him saying in derision, Hail king of the Jews. Prayers follow for the Pope, for all the clergy, and holy people of God (formerly for the Emperor also) and catechumens who are to receive baptism on the day following. Having prayed for all members of the church, we then pray for heretics and schismatics, that God may deign to "deliver them from all errors, and bring them back to their holy mother the catholic and apostolic church"; and these petitions are followed by others for the conversion of Jews and Pagans[86].

|Exposition of the cross: ancient crucifixes and crosses.

|Adoration of the cross: its antiquity.

When these prayers are ended[87] the officiating Cardinal takes off his chasuble, and going to the epistle-side of the altar receives from the deacon the crucifix[88] covered with a black veil. Then turning towards the people, and uncovering the upper part of the crucifix, he sings, Behold the wood of the cross, on which hung the salvation of the world; in singing which words he is joined by two tenor-voices from the choir. The choir answers, Come, let us adore[89]. The Pope and all others kneel, except the Cardinal celebrant, who advances nearer to the middle of the altar, and uncovers the right arm of the crucifix, and repeats the same words in a higher tone, and again in a still higher tone before the middle of the altar, where he uncovers the whole cross. The choir answers as before, and all except the celebrant kneel each time the words are repeated. The Cardinal then places the crucifix on a rich cushion lying on the steps of the altar[90].

|Trisagion.

I observed above, that it was formerly customary for the Pope and all others to walk bare-footed in the procession of this day, as others royal personages have done; for instance, S. Louis of France, S. Elisabeth of Hungary, and others. Thus to be barefooted was a sign of mourning (1 Sam. XV, 30. Jer. II, 25) among the Jews. Their priests were without shoes at their functions, in token of reverence (Exod. III, 5. Jos. V, 15). Some memorial of this practice is preserved in the present custom of taking off the shoes of the principal persons who revere and kiss the cross on this day. The Pope's shoes are taken off by an *Ajutante di Camera*, His cope by acolythes (*Votanti di Segnatura*), and afterwards His Holiness then makes three profound genuflections before the crucifix, gradually approaching nearer to it, and then kisses it in token of his love for Him, who died upon it for our salvation[91]. He also empties a purse, containing an offering of 100 *scudi d'oro*, into a silver basin near the crucifix. When the Pope is about to make the first genuflection, the choir begins to sing the *improperii*, the sentiments of which, and the chant composed by Palestrina [92], are admirably adapted to the pathetic ceremony. In them God enumerates the unparalleled benefits which he lavished upon the Jews, and the atrocious crimes by which they repaid Him. At the end of each *improperium* or reproach, the Trisagion is sung by one choir in Greek, and in Latin by another "Holy God! Holy strong one! Holy immortal, have mercy on us"[93]. The Pope then returns to his throne; he resumes his previous vestments and reads the *improperii* from the Missal held as usual by an assist. bishop kneeling. The Cardinal celebrant and all the other members of the sacred college, after their shoes have been taken off, assisted by the *Ceremonieri* revere and kiss the crucifix in the same manner as the Pope has done; and each of them leaves an offering of a *scudo d'oro* according to an ancient custom.[94] When they return to their places, their shoes are put on by their respective *camerieri*, who afterwards leave the chapel. The patriarchs and bishops assistant and non-assistant and the generals of religious orders without shoes, and all the other prelates etc. wearing their shoes, *adore* and kiss the cross in like manner, observing the same order as in going to receive palms on the preceding sunday; and they also make their offerings before the cross. When the sacred college has finished the *adoration*, the choir having ended the *improperii* sings the anthem *Crucem tuam*, the psalm *Deus misereatur nostri*, the hymn *Pange lingua gloriosi lauream certaminis*[95] etc. Towards the end of this beautiful ceremony the candles are lighted, the deacon spreads out the corporal[96] as usual, placing the purificator near it. He then respectfully takes the cross, and places it on the altar amid the candlesticks.

|*Chant of Pange lingua etc.*

A procession, arranged like that of the preceding day, now goes to the Pauline chapel. Assisted as usual by the first Card. priest, the Pope kneels and incenses the B. Sacrament three times. *M. Sagrista* delivers the B. Sacrament to the Cardinal celebrant, who presents it to the Pope; His Holiness covers it with the end of the veil placed over his shoulders[97] and the procession returns to the Sixtine chapel [98]. In the mean time the choir sings the hymn *"Vexilla Regis prodeunt"*. When the Pope arrives at the altar, he delivers the B. Sacrament to the Card. Celebrant, who places it on the altar. His Holiness then incenses it and returns to his throne.

During the procession the crucifix on the altar of the Sixtine chapel is removed, and a larger cross containing a considerable relic of the true cross is substituted for it. This relic was sent to Pope Leo the Great in the 5th century by Juvenal Bishop of Jerusalem. It was lost, but found again by Pope Sergius I in 687: it was stolen at the sack of Rome in 1527, and removed from its case of silver: however it was recovered by Clement VII, who ordered the rich cross, in which it is at present preserved, to be made: in 1730 it was again stolen but recovered once more by Clement XII. At the close of the last century, though the candlesticks, and the statues of the Apostles belonging to the papal chapel were lost, this cross was preserved. In 1840 His present Holiness Gregory XVI ordered it to be again exposed to the public veneration in the Sixtine chapel: He gave it to the charge of the chapter of S. Peter's, who deliver it to *M. Sagrista* on Good-friday morning: and it remains in the Sixtine chapel till the end of Tenebrae on that day. Moroni *Cappelle Pontificie etc.*

The *Mass* of the *Presanctified*, as it is called, is next celebrated; Card. Tommasi, following S. Cesarius of Arles, calls it the office, and not the mass of good-Friday; for mass, strictly speaking, is not offered up on this day, since no consecration takes place, and the B. Sacrament is received by the celebrant under the form of bread alone, as it could not be preserved with safety under the form of wine[99].

|Mass of the Pre-Sanctified.

The Card. Celebrant places the B. Sacrament on the paten[100] and thence on the corporal. In the meantime the deacon puts wine into the chalice, and the subdeacon water, which however are neither blessed or consecrated[101] on this day. The cardinal then places the chalice on the altar, and the deacon covers it with the *palla* or pall (a small square piece of linen, which serves to prevent flies etc. from falling into it). The Cardinal incenses the offerings and the altar, washes his hands, and recites the *Orate Fratres* and Our Father. All then kneel to adore the blessed Sacrament, which he raises over the paten. He divides it as usual, but without saying any prayer [102], into three parts, putting one of them into the chalice. Striking his breast, and acknowledging his own unworthiness, he receives communion, taking the sacred host, and afterwards the consecrated particle with the wine in the chalice [103]. He then receives the ablution, washes his hands, and returns to the sacristy with the sacred ministers.

|Vespers.

Anciently on fasting days nothing was allowed to be eaten till sunset; and Vespers used therefore to be said before dinner: now that the one meal allowed on such days may be eaten as early as noon, the ancient practice of saying Vespers before dinner is still preserved. Vespers are therefore sung immediately after the mass of the Presanctified: they consist of the Our Father and Hail Mary said in secret, of five psalms with their anthems, and the

Magnificat with its anthem. At the verse 'Christ became obedient unto death', all kneel down to adore Him, and the *Miserere* and the usual prayer are recited, but without the solemnity of Tenebrae[104].

|*Tenebræ.*

|*Principal relics.*

In the afternoon at Tenebrae, the office, being that of Holy Saturday anticipated as usual, refers to the repose of the body of our blessed Lord in the tomb. When it is finished, the Pope wearing his stole, and the Cardinals having taken off their *cappe*, go to S. Peter's in procession, accompanied by the Papal *Anticamera segreta*, the guards and others, to venerate the relics of the Cross, the Lance, and the *Volto Santo*, which are shewn by the Canons from the gallery above the statue of S. Veronica [105]. The Pope meantime, and the Cardinals and others arranged on each side of Him, remain kneeling. The Pontifical cross is borne as usual before the Pope, when going to S. Peter's by an *Uditore di Rota*, and when returning to His apartments by His cross-bearer who is one of His chaplains.

|*Grounds of belief in relics.*

Catholics are bound to believe with divine faith only those doctrines, which the church defines to be doctrines taught by God; and hence with regard to particular images or relics or miracles, concerning which Christ has taught nothing, they believe them to be genuine or reject them, according to the evidence which accompanies them. We shall therefore briefly examine what evidence there is in favour of the relics in question.

|*I. Relic of the cross.*

1. The relic of the cross was placed here in 1629 by Urban VIII; but it was formed of some pieces taken from the churches of S. Anastasia and S. Croce in Gerusalemme. The Jews were accustomed to bury the instruments of punishment in or near the place where the persons executed were buried; but on this subject I must content myself with referring to Baronius, Calmet, Menochius, Gretser etc. who cite the Rabbins in proof of this assertion. Now according to the ancient historians, Eusebius, Sozomen and Socrates: the Emperor Adrian erected a temple of Venus over the tomb of the God of purity, after he had covered it with a great quantity of rubbish. Helen the saintly mother of the emperor Costantine, after many searches (according to Eusebius in his life of that emperor) at length discovered the sacred tomb, in which was found, according to Sozomen, the inscription placed over the cross by Pilate, "Jesus of Nazareth, King of the Jews"[106]. Near the tomb in another part of the cave were found three crosses: but here a difficulty arose on which of these three was our Saviour crucified? At the suggestion of Macarius Bp. of Jerusalem, a woman at the point of death, as Ruffinus, Socrates, Theodoret,

Sozomen and Nicephorus relate; or a dead man, according to Paulinus and Severus Sulpicius, was brought to the spot, and restored to health or to life, when placed on *one* of the three crosses. If we consider, that it is related in the 2nd book of Kings c, XIII, that when some persons "were burying a man, they cast the body into the sepulchre of Eliseus. And when it had touched the bones of Eliseus, the man came to life and stood up on his feet," we may not be unwilling to admit the possibility or probability, that such a miracle may have occurred at the sepulchre of the God of Eliseus. Besides the authors whom I have mentioned, this history is attested by S. Ambrose, S. Chrysostom, and S. Cyril of Jerusalem. This great bishop and Eusebius lived at the time when the event is said to have happened: the other writers lived not long after, and Ruffinus and Theodoret passed part of their lives in Syria. The same historians mention, that S. Helen divided the Cross into three parts, one she left in Jerusalem, another she sent to Costantine, according to the author of the life of Pope Sylvester published by Pope Damasus towards the close of the 6th cent.; and the third she reserved for herself, to Rome. She placed the last mentioned piece in the Sessorian Basilica, called also the Basilica of Helen, because erected by her, in the Horti Variani: hence is derived its title of S. Croce in Gerusalemme. On this subject additional information may be found in the work of the late Padre De Corrieris, De Sessorianis praecipius D.N.J.C. reliquiis, in Trombelli De cultu SSrum and Ben. XIV. De festis. From Santa Croce a piece of the cross was taken to S. Peter's, and is one of the relics shewn on good friday. Even in the fourth century S. Cyril of Jerusalem testifies, that particles of the true cross had been sent to every Christian country.

|2. *of the lance.*

2. The lance also with which our divine Saviour's side was pierced, was found by S. Helen, as the Bollandists shew: and it was preserved in Jerusalem, as S. Gregory of Tours and our venerable Bede observe: but towards the end of the 6th cent., the iron part of it was transfered to Costantinople; of this the point was placed in the imperial palace; the other part in the church of S. Sophia, and afterwards in that of S. John. William of Tyre and Anna Comnena mention it as existing there in the 11th and 12th centuries. Towards the close of the 13th century the point of the lance with other relics passed into the possession of S. Louis of France: the other part of the lance still remained at S. John's in Constantinople, as Buondelmount, who saw it, bears witness. When Mahomet subdued Costantinople, he preserved all the relics, as Theodore cited by Benedict XIV relates in his history of the Turks, and his son Bajazet sent an ambassador with the relics of the lance to Pope Innocent VIII, in order to induce his Holiness not to protect Zizimus, who disputed with him the succession to the Turkish throne. The Pope

received it with great reverence, and placed it in the Vatican. As some suspicion was entertained about the veracity of the Turkish ambassador, Benedict XIV, as he mentions in his very learned work on the Canonisation of the Saints, from which I have extracted this account, sent for an exact cast of the point preserved at Paris, which perfectly corresponded with the piece preserved in the Vatican; and thus were confirmed the assertion of the Turk[107].

3. *Volto Santo.*

3. As for the *Volto Santo*, or image of our Saviour it was placed in an Oratory of the Vatican Basilica by John VII as long ago as 707, as may be seen in Marlinetti, Dei pregii della Basilica Vat. Who S. Veronica or Berenice was, who is said to have wiped our Saviour's face with the handkerchief is another question, as Benedict XIV observes, to whom and to Marlinetti I shall content myself with referring. It appears that this ancient likeness of our Saviour was afterwards kept at S. Spirito: six Roman noblemen had the care of it; and to each of them was confided on of the six keys, with which it was locked up. They enjoyed various privileges, and among others, says an ancient MS. Chronicle quoted by Cancellieri, "havevano questi sei ogni anno, da Santo Spirito, due vacche in die S. Spiritus le quali se magnavano li con gran festa". In 1410 the *Volto Santo* was carried back to S. Peter's, where it has ever since remained[108].

Reflections.

The Council of Trent, in the 25th Session, teaches that veneration and honour are due to relics of the Saints, and that they and other sacred monuments are honoured by the faithful not without utility. We all honour the memorials of the great, of the wise and of the brave; who has not venerated the oak of a Tasso or the house of a Shakespeare? While *We* revere the relics of a Borromeo at Milan, of a Francois de Sales at Annecy, of a Luigi Gonzaga, a Filippo Neri, a Camillo de Lellis at Rome, others respect the chair and table of Wickliffe at Lutterworth, or the room of Luther at Eisenach. If infidels unite in paying homage to the house of the impious *philosopher* of Ferney, let all Christians, however they may be otherwise unhappily divided, join in shewing their respect for the image of their Saviour, and for those instruments which touched his sacred body, and were sanctified by his precious blood. O let them gaze with reverential awe on that lance which entering into his adorable side drew from it blood and water, and on that cross to which he was nailed and on which he died for our salvation. The early Christians, our forefathers in the faith, manifested great respect for the bodies and the blood of the martyrs, because they were faithful *followers* of Christ. Thus, in the letter of the faithful of Smyrna preserved by Eusebius, they mention that they gathered up the bones of their bishop Polycarp, (a disciple of S. John the Apostle) "more precious than pearls, and more tried than gold, and buried them. In this place, God willing", say they "we shall meet and celebrate with joy and gladness the birthday of this martyr". SS. Praxedes and Pudentiana, and many other devout females used to collect the blood of the martyrs with sponges and cloths, as if they feared that one drop of it should be lost. Read the poems of Prudentius, observe the phials of blood[109] placed before the martyrs' tombs in the catacombs, and you will not doubt the truth of such assertions[110]. The shadow of Peter, the handkerchiefs which had touched the body of Paul, could cure diseases, as the Scripture witnesseth; but here are the relics of a greater than Paul, of a greater than Peter: O then let us kneel, and love, and venerate them; for they were closely united to Him who is the author and object of our faith, the only foundation of our hope, the centre and the consummation of our love.

Recapitulation.

It does not fall within my plan to speak of the devotion of the three hours of agony, practised on this day in many churches, as at the Gesù, S. Lorenzo in Damaso etc. or of that which is practised after the *Ave Maria* at S. Marcello, Caravita etc. or of the elegies recited by the Arcadian pastors over their Redeemer. Let us rather briefly recapitulate with Morcelli the principal ceremonies of the day: Station at S. Croce; service in the Sixtine chapel, the veneration of the Cross; the B. Sacrament carried thither in procession from the Pauline chapel, Mass of the Presanctified and Vespers. In the afternoon Tenebræ, and veneration of the relics at S. Peter's.

Footnote 82: (return)

See a MS. Apamean Pontifical ap. Marthene T. 3, p. 132, Benedict Canon of S. Peter's in his *Ordo Romanus*, Marangoni, *Istoria dell antichissimo Oratorio o Cappella di S. Lorenzo nel Patriarchio Lateranense*. Roma 1747. S. Louis of France used to walk barefooted on this day to the churches, praying and giving abundant alms, as did also William, king of the Romans. (Chronicon Erphordense ad ann. 1252), S. Elisabeth of Hungary used to devote the day to similar acts of piety, walking barefooted and in the dress of a poor woman to the churches, and there making her humble offerings at the altars, and distributing copious alms. On her practices of piety during holy-week see her life by Le Cte de Montalembert c. 9.

Footnote 83: (return)

The Corporal, which was anciently much longer than at present, was spread in this manner at all masses before the offertory. See Cancellieri, De Secretariis T. I, Fleury, Moeurs des Chretiens.

Footnote 84: (return)

The lessons, the prayer, and the passion are found in the ancient ordo Gelasianus for this day.

Footnote 85: (return)

According to the Gelasian Sacramentary all were to genuflect at the prayer for the Jews, as well as at the other prayers; not so according to the Gregorian Sacramentary.

Footnote 86: (return)

"God our Saviour", says S. Paul (1 Tim. II, 4) "wishes all men to be saved, and to come to the knowledge of the truth". The Catholic church is animated by the same spirit of charity, as the admirable prayers of this day might alone prove. If she teaches exclusive salvation. Christ taught the same "He that believeth and is baptised shall be saved: he that believeth not shall be condemned" Mark XVI, 26. We cannot therefore consistently accuse the church of want of charity, when she proclaims the general conditions of salvation, without at the same time charging Christ himself, who first taught them, with the same fault. True charity desires the salvation of all but she warns others of their danger; and does not cruelly conceal it from them till it is too late.

Footnote 87: (return)

After these prayers the faithful used anciently to leave the church, and the Priests to go to their own churches, to perform the ceremonies till the evening-service: so that what follows was then a totally distinct service. See Sacram S. Gregorii, ant. Ord. Roman, etc. ap. Martene lib. IV, c. 23.

Footnote 88: (return)

It would appear, that, before Costantine abolished the punishment of malefactors on the cross, the Christians, who well knew with S. Paul that Christ crucified was to the Jews a stumbling-block, and to the gentiles foolishness', prudently abstained from representing our Saviour nailed to the cross, and used rather to depict a lamb with a cross near it, of which instances may he seen in Rork's Hierurgia p. 520. The first mention of the *crucifix* in the church is believed to occur in the poem titled *De Passione Domini* referred to the fourth century. That the use of the sign and the image of the *cross* was much more ancient and very prevalent among Christians will appear from the following facts. "At every step and movement" says Tertullian (in the early part of the third century) "whenever we come in or go out, when we dress and wash ourselves, at table, when lights are brought in, whether we are lying or sitting down; whatever we are doing, we mark our foreheads with the sign of the cross". Eusebius mentions that Constantine placed a magnificent cross De Vit. Const. I. 3. In the fourth century in his palace S. John Chrysostom in one of his eloquent homilies observes "Every where the symbol of the cross is present to us. We inscribe it very diligently on our houses, and walls, and doors, and brows, and thoughts". S. Basil (De Spirit. S. ad Amphilochium c. 27.) derives the sign of the cross from Apostolic tradition. That this custom universally prevailed among Christians might be proved from S. Jerome, from the historian Socrates and others, and from monuments of the early Christians still preserved in Egypt: but why travel so far? we have only lo look around us in the catacombs, or in the Vatican Museum and Library. The cross is the chosen, the beloved sign of Christians; they repeated it a thousand times on their lamps, on their rings, on their cups and sacred vessels, that they might have the sign of their redemption ever before their eyes, they kissed it at the hour of their death, and had it marked on their tomb, as a sign of their hope of salvation. No sooner had peace shone upon the church, than crosses were erected on high roads, and in many places of public resort: and would to God that those sacred ancient monuments, which once adorned our own country, bore public testimony to the faith of its inhabitants, and recalled to the minds of passers-by the sufferings of their Saviour, had not been too rudely treated in the first heat of religious and political frenzy!

For some ancient representations of the cross see the learned work of Dr. Rock on the mass. I shall content myself with noticing an interesting instance, which he has not mentioned. At Pompeii the house of Pansa, as it is called, is one of the most remarkable yet excavated on account of its extent and regularity. Some parts of it were used as shops, and appear to have been let out, (as is still the custom in some palaces of Rome): for they have no communication with the body of the building. Between two parts thus separated is an entrance from a side street to the peristyle or open court surrounded by columns; and on the pier between the two doors is, or rather was a painting representing one of the guardian-serpents or tutelary deities, who were sometimes represented under that form, as we occasionally see at Pompeii, and as we learn from Virgil (lib.) V. Hence as we see in Titus' baths and are informed by Persius, a place was considered sacred, in which serpents were painted. Indeed these reptiles became such favourites, that, according to Seneca, they used to creep upon the tables amid the cups: and some ladies so far overcame natural prejudices, as to place real serpents, if not boas, round their necks, to cool them, instead of using artificial boas to warm themselves. "Si gelidum nectit collo Glacilla draconem" says Martial. Before the serpent painted in Pansa's house is or was a projecting brick intended to support a lamp: the painting in consequence of its situation could be seen only by persons within the house: but upon the opposite wall there is or was a cross worked in bas relief upon a panel of white stucco, so situated as to be visible to all persons passing. It had the form of a Latin cross, which, we may observe, as well as the Greek cross: is found upon ancient Christian monuments; though of course we cannot bring forward other instances so ancient as the monument in question. (See Rock p. 516). "It is hard to conceive", says the learned Mazois, "that the same man should bow at once before the cross of Christ, and pay homage to Janus, Ferculus, Limetinus, Cardia, the deities of the threshold, and the hinges of doors. Perhaps at this time the cross was of a meaning unknown except to those who had embraced the Christian faith, which, placed here among the symbols of paganism, as if in testimony of gratitude, informed the faithful, that the truth had here found an asylum with a poor man, under the safeguard of all the popular superstitions". So far Mazois, whose opinion is embraced by the author of the interesting work on Pompeii published by the society for promoting useful knowledge: but is it not probable, I may ask, or rather is it not certain that, at that early period, while some members of the same family were pagans, others were Christians? it is not then surprising if in the same house we find both Christian and Pagan emblems: we may suppose, that some such persons may have been inmates of the same house as Mr. Bulwer's pagan gladiator Lydon and his Christian father Medon. Pompeii was overwhelmed by ashes in the year of Christ 79: and if Vesuvius still occasionally lay waste the surrounding country, we are indebted to it for the preservation not only of a thousand classical monuments, but also of a representation of the cross of Christ, which cannot be of a much later date than the time of the destruction of Jerusalem.

Footnote 89: (return)

St. Helen discovered the cross on which Christ suffered, and erected a church in Jerusalem, in which it was deposited. "The bishop of that city every year, at the season of the paschal solemnity, exhibits it to be *adored* by the people, after he himself has first performed his act of profound veneration". S. Paulinus of Nola, A.D. 430, ep. 11 ad Sever. "In the middle of Lent, the life-giving wood of the venerable cross is usually exposed for *adoration*". S. Sophronius patriarch of Jerusalem in 639. (Orat. in Exalt. Crucis). From this custom of the church of Jerusalem probably arose that of the Roman church, in which a crucifix, containing a particle of the true cross, was publicly venerated on good Friday. In the Sacramentary of pope Gelasius (A.D. 402) we read in an account of the ceremonies of this day "The priest comes before the altar, adoring the Lord's cross and kissing it—all adore the holy cross and communicate". This ceremony is mentioned also in the Antiphonary of S. Gregory the great and the ancient *Ordo Romanus.* Flecte genu, lignumque crucis venerabile adora, says Lactantius. See bishop Poynter's Christianity p. 151. Of the Greeks Leo Allatius relates that "on good-friday, while they accompany as it were Christ himself to the tomb, they lead round through the cities and *adore* the sculptured body of Christ". De consensu utriusque Eccl. lib. 5. c. 15. The Syrians also practise this ceremony, as we learn from documents published by Card. Borgia and Nairon. This rite is called the *adoration* of the cross. Let us not forget what is said in the Book of Common Prayer in the solemnization of Matrimony "With this ring I thee wed; with my body I thee *worship*". Such words of doubtful signification must be interpreted from the doctrine of the church which adopts them. Hanc veniam petimusque damusque vicissim. Now the word *adorare* used in our liturgy (derived from *ad* and *ora,* because persons when *adoring* used to put their right hand to their mouth; Plin. I. 28, c. 2. Apuleius in Apolog.) signifies not only to pay divine worship, but also to venerate and even to salute. Thus from the instances collected in Forcellini's Lexicon we may select the following: "Primo autem septimum Germanici consulatum adoravi". Stat in præf i. 4 Silv. Imo cum gemitu populum sic adorat: Apulei. lib 2. Metam. The doctrine of the catholic church on this subject is as usual clear and decided. The twenty-fifth session of the Council of Trent decreed as follows: "The holy synod commands all bishops, and others sustaining the duty and care of teaching, that they should diligently instruct the faithful concerning the legitimate use of images according to the custom of the catholic and apostolic church received from the commencement of christianity, and the consent of the holy fathers, and decrees of the sacred councils, teaching them ... that the images of Christ; of the Virgin mother of God, and other saints, are to be had and retained especially in churches, and that due honour and veneration are to be given them: not that any divinity or virtue is believed to exist in them for which they are to be worshipped, or that any thing is to be asked from them, or that confidence is to be placed in images, as was formerly done by the Gentiles, who used to place their hope in idol; but because the honour which is given to them is referred to the prototypes which they represent; so that by the images which we kiss, and before which we uncover our heads and bow our bodies, we adore Christ, and venerate the Saints, whose likeness they bear: this has been decreed against the opposers of images by the decrees of councils, especially of the second synod of Nice. And let the bishops diligently teach, that by the histories of the mysteries of our redemption expressed in pictures or other likenesses the people are instructed and confirmed in commemorating and assiduously venerating articles of faith, and that from all sacred images a great fruit is derived, not only because the people are admonished of the benefits and gifts conferred on them by Christ, but also because God's miracles through the saints, and salutary examples are laid before the eyes of the faithful, that they may return thanks for them to God, and may compose their life and manners to an imitation of the saints, and may be excited to adore and love God and cherish piety". The council then gives directions for the extirpation of any abuses which may creep in. These words, by which our faith and practice are regulated, are too clear to need comment, and sufficiently justify catholics from the foolish and calumnious charge of idolatry. The true Catholic practice is well expressed in a work attributed to Alcuin "We prostrate our bodies before the cross, and our souls before the Lord: we venerate the cross by which we have been redeemed, and we supplicate Him who redeemed us".

Footnote 90: (return)

This rite is described in the Ordo Romanus XIV with the same ceremonies. It is first mentioned in the Ordo XI of the Canon Benedict.

Footnote 91: (return)

We kiss and press to our hearts the pictures of those whom we love, and shall we think it sinful to kiss the image of Him, who for love of us humbled himself even to the death of the cross? Oh! let each one of us rather exclaim with S. Paul "God forbid that I should glory save in the cross of our Lord Jesus Christ, by whom the world is crucified to me and I to the world" (Gal. VI): or in the words attributed to S. Andrew when he was going to be crucified "Hail precious cross, that hast been consecrated by the body of my Lord, and adorned with his limbs as with rich jewels. Oh good cross, that hast received beauty from our Lord's limbs, I have ardently loved thee, long have I desired and sought thee; now thou art found by me and made ready for my longing soul". Act. S. Andreæ.

Footnote 92: (return)

"The greatest glory" says Baini "was deservedly obtained by *Pierluigi* on account of the *improperii*, and the hymn *Crux fidelis* which he set to music for 8 voices divided into two choirs, and which were sung for the first time by the choir of the Lateran basilica on good Friday in the year 1560: by them *fece sbalordire arte e natura*. Pius IV demanded them for the use of the apostolic chapel, and, after he had heard them, declared that Palestrina had surpassed his expectations. These *improperii* are still sung and will ever be sung in the apostolic chapel" Baini, Mem. storic. di Giovanni Pierluigi da Palestrina 1. p. 64.

Footnote 93: (return)

This hymn is frequently sung in the Greek and Oriental church. Renaudot T. I, p. 70. According in the Menologium Græcum and S. John Damascen it was first used in the reign of Theodosius, when public supplications were offered to heaven during a terrible earthquake at Costantinople. This Palmer admits, I, 64. It is still said in Greek, in which it was originally composed, as well as in Latin, in the Roman church. See Goar in notis ad Rituale Græc.

Footnote 94: (return)

In the Ordo Romanus XII, Ap. 1, de Presbyterio, it is prescribed that "according to ancient custom whatever is offered upon the cross ought to belong to the *schola* (or company)" of the cross: in the Ordo XIV, that it belongs to the *Sagrista*. The sum collected is at present the perquisite of M. Sagrista and the two principal Masters of ceremonies. These offerings were customary also in other churches, and in particular at Paris.

Footnote 95: (return)

Baini observes, that the chant of this hymn is one of the few instances of *rhythmical* chant preserved by uninterrupted *tradition* in the papal chapel and adorned with the ancient ornaments. (See his Saggio sopra l'indentità dei ritmi musicale e poetico. Firenze, 1820). "The chant of that hymn" says Eximano (quoted by Baini, Mem. Stor.) is a true plain chant, that is, a chant of unison, such as it is found in all choral books: but the mode of singing it in the pontifical chapel makes it appear different from what is sung in other churches—Above all, the distribution of the notes, which are sung (not of those which are written) adapted to express the length and shortness of the syllables which compose the rhythm of the hymn, ought to be studied. "Se si dà quell'inno ad un maestro di cappella per metterlo in musica concertata ed in *battuta sensibile*, verrà subito distrutto il *ritmo*, e se la cantilena della cappella pontif. si scrive in battuta, si vedranno cadere nel *battere* alcune sillabe brevi, senza pregiudizio della loro quantità". Dubbio di D. Antonio Eximeno sopra il saggio fondamentale pratico di contrappunto del R.P.M. Martini. Roma, 1773.

Footnote 96: (return)

The corporal is a square piece of linen so called, because the Corpus or body of

Christ is placed on it. S. Isidore of Pelusium in the beginning of the 5th century says, that the white linen cloth, which is spread under the divine gifts, is the clean linen cloth of Joseph of Arimathea: "for we, sacrificing the bread of proposition on the linen cloth, without doubt find like him the body of Christ": it was anciently much larger than it is at present. The purificator is a small towel, which serves to wipe the chalice and the hands and mouth of the priest, after he has received the B. Sacrament.

Footnote 97: (return)

The veil is used from reverence to the B. Sacrament: on an ancient mosaic on one of the arches of S. Prassede, a person is represented enveloped in it, holding a sacred vessel apparently intended to contain the B. Sacrament. Ciampini, Vet. mon. T. 2.

Footnote 98: (return)

According to the Gelasian Sacramentary, "the deacons go to the *sacrarium* and walk in procession with the body and blood of the Lord, which remained from the preceding day": with it the most ancient Ordo Romanus ad usum monasteriorum agrees.

Footnote 99: (return)

In the fourth century Pope Innocent I in his epistle to Decentius assigns as a reason, why the holy sacrifice is not offered up on this day, the example of the apostles who, concealing themselves for fear of the Jews, spent this and the following day in fasting and mourning for the death of their master, and were thus debarred from the holy mysteries. During the whole of Lent the Greek church still celebrates, towards evening, only the mass of the presanctified, except on Saturdays and Sundays, and on the feast of the Annunciation, when the ordinary mass is offered up. This is one of the ancient instances of communion under one kind; for, as Leo Allatius observes, either it is received under the form of bread alone, or if some drops of the sacred blood were sprinkled on the host, all the species of wine have disappeared before communion. (De utriusque Ecclesiæ consensione, p. 875). Neither in the Latin or the Greek church is the mass of the pre-sanctified a *Missa sicca* or dry mass: in which not only the consecration, but also the communion, and all those prayers which are said over the holy Eucharist, used to be omitted. See Durandus in Rationali c. 1. This is the only day in the year on which mass is not offered up in the Latin church, and even on it the priest communicates: on holy Saturday mass is said, but the priest alone communicates: on all other days all the faithful may and many do communicate, either during mass or before or after it according to circumstances. Palmer having quoted a passage from Bona, in which the Cardinal regrets that communion, as well as other rites to which the mass is not essential, is often delayed till after the mass is ended, subjoins the following ejaculation. "Would that they who communicate with the Roman church were not too timid or too lukewarm to return to the practice of the primitive church in this and many other respects". Orig. Liturg. vol. 2, p. 154. Now in the primitive church the faithful, and even those in health, used to communicate not only during mass, but also at other times, as is evident from the office of the presanctified, at which, according to the Gelasian sacramentary, all present communicated, as well as from the numerous ancient instances of communion under one kind mentioned in the preceding chapter; for in these cases it was not received during the mass, and many of them are cases of "*persons in health*". In the same page Mr. Palmer observes that "*during all the primitive ages* the whole body of the faithful communicated at each celebration of the liturgy". Now has the church of England preserved this "practice of the primitive church"? So far is this from being the case, that Palmer considers her *ordinary* office as a "*Missa sicca*; or dry service" p. 164, in which there is neither consecration or communion, and the earliest notice of which occurs in the writings of Petrus Cantor (A.D. 1200), according to Palmer's own admission, ibid. Even on those few days in the year when she admits her children to communion, her ministers generally consider that they make an oblation only of bread and wine, and not of the body and blood of Christ, whereas, whatever Palmer or the Tracts for the Times may say to the contrary, we are prepared to prove from the *very liturgies*, which the former cites, that in the mass there is an oblation not merely of bread and wine but also of the body and blood of Christ; and accordingly even the author of Tract 81, vol. 4, admits, p. 61, that "the real point of difference between the primitive church and modern views is whether there be in this oblation a *mystery* or no". It is truly lamentable that men of learning should falsely accuse the Roman church of departure from primitive discipline in a matter of so little comparative importance as the precise *time* when communion is to be received, while they themselves must acknowledge, that they have *abolished communion* itself as well as *consecration* on *nearly* all the days of the year, and that they have reduced the oblation of the mass from a '*mystery*' and a '*venerable, tremendous and unbloody sacrifice*' (Palmer vol. 2, p. 84) to an offering of bread and wine. They have thus deprived their followers of the inestimable fruits of communion enumerated by Christ in the gospel—yet these forsooth are the men who charge Catholics with a departure from primitive practice. How many other *primitive practices* mentioned in this work have been abolished by the church of England!

Footnote 100: (return)

This plate, which is of gold or silver-gilt, resembles *in form* the patera used in the ancient sacrifices, and generally represented together with the *prefericulum* on sepulchral monuments dedicated to the Manes.

Footnote 101: (return)

The wine is sanctified, but is not consecrated, either by the particle of the sacred host, or by the recital of the *Pater noster*, as has been shewn by Mabillon, (Museum Ital.) Bossuet, and other authors quoted by Benedict XIV. The wine and water represent the blood and water, which flowed on this day from Christ's body. See Act. Coer. p. 54. Whenever priests *say Mass*, they receive under both kinds, in compliance with the command of Christ "Drink ye all of this" which words as well as those others, "Do this in commemoration of me" were addressed to the apostles and their successors.

Footnote 102: (return)

According to the direction of the Gelasian sacramentary, the *Pax Domini etc.* is not said on this day.

Footnote 103: (return)

"As the communion," says Mabillon "is of the nature of a sacred banquet, it consists of food and drink; hence the other part of the banquet, viz. drink, was supplied by wine, mixed with water, but sanctified by a particle of the B. Sacrament" See for the service of this day a MS. Pontifical of the church of Apamea in Syria ap. Martene t. 3, p. 132. It is found with little variation also in the Gelasian Sacramentary, in a very ancient *Ordo Romanus*, and some MSS. cited by Martene. In the Roman church, as Amalarius was informed by the Roman archdeacon "at the station no one communicated". In many other churches there was general communion; this is prescribed by the church during this holy season.

Footnote 104: (return)

In many churches the crucifix used to be solemnly placed in the *sepulchre* after the Vespers. See the Sarum and other missals, ap. Martene t. 3, p. 139.

Footnote 105: (return)

So jealously are these relics kept, that even sovereigns cannot go up where they are preserved, without being first appointed Canons of the Basilica. The Emperor Frederic III, and afterwards Ladislaus son of the king of Poland, and Cosimo III grand-duke of Tuscany went up dressed as Canons of St. Peter's.

Footnote 106: (return)

The learned professor Sholz after his return from Palestine defended in a dissertation the genuineness of this tomb against Dr. Clark's objections: if it be within the walls of the modern city of Jerusalem, it was certainly outside the ancient walls.

Footnote 107: (return)

The lance preserved at Nuremberg resembles in form that of St. Peter's, but is made of common iron, united with a part of one of the nails of the cross.

Footnote 108: (return)

These relics are shewn to the people on holy-Wednesday after the matins of Tenebræ; on Thursday and Friday several times in the day: on holy Saturday morning after mass: on Easter Sunday after the Pontifical mass: on Easter Monday, and a few other festivals.

Footnote 109: (return)

The opinion of Röstell (Beschreibung der Stadt Rom, B. I, p. 400) that these phials contained the blessed eucharist under the form of wine, if admitted, would form a new proof of the real and permanent presence of Christ's blood in the B. Sacrament; yet it is a novel, unsupported, and untenable conjecture. Some of the ancient Christian Fathers complain, it is true, of the abuse of burying the eucharist with the deceased under the form of bread; but the phials of blood have been found with so many bodies, that we cannot reasonably suppose the custom to have been an abuse: and who among the ancients mentions that the eucharist was ever buried with them under the form of *wine*? That the palm-branch or crown accompanied by these phials of blood are authentic signs of martyrdom, see Raoul-Rochette's Memoires sur les pierre sepulcrales, t. XIII des Mem. de l'Academie, p. 210, 217. On one of the phials mentioned by Röstell was found the inscription Sanguis Saturnini.

Footnote 110: (return)

In the Vatican Library is a small relic-case, marked with the monogram, of great simplicity and consequent antiquity. There is another of ivory, adorned with bas-reliefs of the resuscitation of Lazarus, Christ's apprehension etc. Plainer, Bescher. der Stadt Rom. B. 2. See also Rock's Hierurgia Vol. 2, cap 6.

CHAP. VI.

ON THE CEREMONIES OF HOLY-SATURDAY

CONTENTS.

Service of Easter-eve—Ceremonies of holy-saturday-morning—Sixtine chapel. 1. Blessing of the fire and incense-procession; Paschal candle—the deacon sings the *Exultet*—triple candle—2. Baptism administered on this day: communion of children in former times—prophecies—3. The litany: invocation of Saints—change from mourning to rejoicing—High mass: sacred pictures etc.—*Alleluja*—Vespers—end of the mass: mass of Pope Marcellus—Ceremonies at S. John Laterans. Blessing of the font: baptistery—baptism of adults—litanies and confirmation—mass and ordination—Armenian catholics—their liturgy; and high mass on Easter-eve—reflections—Conclusion.

"But now Christ is risen from the dead, the first-fruits of them that sleep". 1 Cor. XV, 20.

|Service of Easter-eve.

I remarked in the last chapter, that anciently mass was not said either on good-friday, or holy-saturday, and I quoted Pope Innocent I, who assigns as a reason the example of the Apostles, who spent those days in mourning for their Master. It was formerly customary to celebrate mass on the night of Easter-eve or holy Saturday. Hence when Tertullian, the oldest Latin Christian writer, endeavoured to dissuade his wife from ever marrying a pagan, in case of his own death, among other arguments he used the following; "Who will tranquilly wait for you, when you are spending the night at the paschal solemnities?" S. Jerome also (in cap. 25 Matt.) says, that according to apostolic tradition, the people did not leave the church on Easter-eve before midnight. This custom continued for many ages; but Hugh of S. Victor in the twelfth century says, that in his time, in order to avoid weakness arising from long fasting, the hour anciently observed was anticipated. The service, which is now performed before noon on holy Saturday, was formerly assigned to the night of Easter-eve: and this anticipation accounts for the occasional mention of night, which it contains, as well as for the early celebration of Christ's resurrection.

|Ceremonies of holy saturday.

The ceremonies of holy saturday-morning may be arranged under three heads: 1st. the blessing of the fire and of the paschal candle: 2nd. the preparation for, and ceremonies of, baptism: 3rd. the litany and mass. All three allude, as we shall see, to the resurrection of Christ, which is the great object of our devotion on this day. In Rome two sanctuaries are the great centres of attraction in the morning, viz. S. John Lateran's on account of the baptism of adults, and the Sixtine chapel, where the service is always beautiful, and particularly on this day. We shall first give an account of the ceremonies observed in the latter, and shall then describe the additional interesting rites of S. John Lateran's.

Sixtine chapel: 1. Blessing of fire and incense.

1. As the missal prescribes, the altar is covered at a convenient hour, and the candles of the altar are not lighted till the beginning of the mass. A light, from which the charcoal for the incense is enkindled, is struck from a flint in the sacristy; where also *M. Sagrista* privately blesses water. The cardinals enter the Sixtine chapel vested in their purple *cappe*: the maces are reversed, as on friday. Meantime in the sacristy the Card. Celebrant wearing a purple cope and mitre, and assisted by the sacred ministers, blesses (as usually with holy water and incense) the fire and the five grains of incense, which are to be fixed in the paschal candle[111].

Procession: Paschal candle.

The Cardinal afterwards changes his cope for a chasuble, which is purple as well as that of the subdeacon; but the deacon, as he is going to bless the Paschal candle[112], wears a white dalmatic. They then enter the Sixtine chapel; where, having put incense into the thurible, the Cardinal remains: but the deacon, the subdeacon who carries the cross, and the other ministers go to the Pauline chapel, whence a procession returns in the following order. After two mace bearers comes an acolythe with the five grains of incense, and another with the thurible; then the subdeacon carrying the cross; and the deacon with a reed, at the top of which are 3 candles united together. At his left hand is a Master of ceremonies with a small candle lighted from the blessed fire, and he is followed by two other acolythes. When the deacon arrives near the door of the *cancellata*, one of the three candles is lighted, and all genuflect, except the subdeacon: the deacon then sings, *Lumen Christi*, the light of Christ, and the choir answers, Thanks be to God. The other two candles are lighted in turn, as the Deacon approaches nearer to the altar; singing the same words each time, but gradually in a higher tone. He then gives the reed to an acolythe; and before he sings the *exultet* or blessing of the Paschal candle, he receives the benediction of the Card. Celebrant, who once more puts incense into the thurible.

The deacon[113] goes to the book, and has the subdeacon on his right hand, and on his left the thurifer and two acolythes, one of whom holds the reed, and the other the plate containing the five grains of incense. All stand, as at the gospel: he incenses the book, and then sings the *Exultet*[114]. After the words *curvat imperia*, he fixes in the candle the five grains of incense in the form of a cross[115]. At the words *"ignis accendit"* he lights the paschal candle with one of the *three* lights[116]. When the blessing, as it is called, is ended, the paschal candle is left lighted near the pulpit and the seats of the Card. deacons, and the triple candle is placed near the altar on the gospel-side[117]. The deacon then takes off his white vestments, puts on others of a purple colour, and joins the Card, celebrant, who accompanied by the ministers takes his seat on *Faldistorio* near the altar on the epistle-side, to hear the prophecies recited.

2. The administration of the Sacrament of Baptism forms an important feature in the ceremonies of this day: indeed anciently it was customary to confer it only on holy-saturday, and the eve of Whit-sunday, except in case of necessity[118]. On these two days those Catechumens who were sufficiently instructed, and also children, used to be baptised[119] by the bishop, and by the bishop of Rome as well as others[120]; and after they had been baptised, they all received Confirmation and the holy Eucharist[121].

The twelve lessons or prophecies read on this day were intended for the instruction of the catechumens; and they are well selected for that purpose, as they contain an account of the creating, the flood, the obedience of Abraham, the deliverance of God's people from their enemies at the red sea, the precept concerning the paschal lamb, the conversion of Ninive, the refusal of the three children to adore Nabuchodonosor's statue, etc. they are twelve in the ancient Gelasian Ordo. They are sung in the Sixtine chapel by members of the papal choir, and are read by the Card. celebrant. After each prophecy the Cardinal standing up sings a prayer: the deacon chants *Flectamus genua* and the subdeacon *Levate* before each, except the last, when the knee is not bent, in order to shew abhorence of the idolatry exacted by Nabuchodonosor for his statue. After the 4th, 8th, and 11th prophecies an appropriate Tract is sung by the choir. Formerly some or all of these prophecies were said in Greek as well as in Latin. (See Cancellieri, *Funz. d. Set. S.* § 4, Martene T. 3. p. 148.). These lesson are recited even where there is no baptismal font, as at the Sixtine chapel. After them follow in S. John Lateran's and other churches the blessing of the font, and in some of them administration of baptism.

3. The litany: invocation of Saints.

Change from mourning to rejoicing.

3. In the papal chapel, immediately after the prophecies, the Celebrant takes off his chasuble, and prostrates himself with the sacred ministers before the altar; all the others also kneel, and two tenor voices from the choir chant in the middle of the chapel the greater litanies, called those of the saints, each petition of which is repeated in the same words by the choir[122]. Before the verse "*Peccatores te rogamus audi nos*" the assistant priest and ministers go to the sacristy, and put on white vestments. Then returning to the chapel they assist the Card. Celebrant to put on his white vestments at his *faldistorio*. The candles are now lighted (at the *Agnus Dei* of the litany, as the Sacramentary of S. Gregory and the Ordo Romanus prescribe); the purple veil which covered the throne and the purple *paliotto* or facing of the altar are removed; and both appear decked in white. The Cardinals assisted by theirs *caudatarii* take off their purple *cappe*, and put on others of scarlet brought in by their respective *camerieri*. The reason of this sudden change from mourning to rejoicing we have already seen: the celebration of Christ's resurrection from the dead is celebrated by anticipation.

High mass.

At the end of the litanies, the Pope (if His Holiness were not present at the preceding ceremonies) enters the chapel, wearing a white cope and a mitre; at the foot of the altar he repeals as usual the beginning of the mass with the Card. Celebrant at His left hand: in the meantime the choir sings solemnly the *Kyrie eleison* etc. (as there is no *Introit* of the Mass, because the people were assembled in the church previously): the Pope goes to His throne, and receives the usual *ubbidienza*; and the other customary ceremonies of high mass in the papal chapel take place (see p. 19 and foll.) with such exceptions as we shall now mention. As soon as the Celebrant commences the *Gloria in excelsis*, the veil is removed from the tapestry over the altar; which represents Christ rising from the dead[123], the cannons of S. Angelo are discharged, the arms are no longer reversed and the bells of the city are tolled, to announce to its faithful inhabitants the resurrection of their Divine Lord.

Alleluja.

After the epistle, sung as usual by the subdeacon, another subdeacon (*Uditore di Rota*) wearing a white *tonacella* or tunic announces at the foot of the throne the joyful tidings to His Holiness[124] by chanting aloud; "*Pater sancte, annuntio vobis gaudium magnum, quod est, Alleluja*": having then kissed the

Pope's foot he returns into the sacristy. This word of joy[125] *Alleluja*, (praise God) which had not been once uttered during the long season of mourning which preceded this solemnity, is now sung thrice by the Celebrant, gradually raising his voice to a higher tone. The choir reechoes it each time, singing it in *contrapunto*, and then chants the verse *Confitemini*, and the tract, which is ordinarily recited in penitential times. Throughout the mass the joy of the church is incomplete; for though Christ has risen from the dead, He has not yet appeared to His disciples, and the light of faith is still overclouded, as Alcuin remarks: hence lights are not carried at the gospel; the Creed, offertory, motetto and *Agnus Dei* are omitted, and the kiss of peace is not given[126]. Merati adds to the cause already assigned the wish to abridge service; particularly on account of the newly-baptised children, who communicated at this mass; and the unusual shortness of the Vespers confirms this opinion.

End of the mass.

After the Celebrant has communicated, Vespers are sung by the choir, in place of the *communion* and postcommunion. They consist of the anthem *Alleluja* repeated three times before and after the short psalm *Laudate Dominion omnes gentes* etc.; of the anthem *Vesper autem sabbati*, which the Celebrant commences and the choir continues; of the *Magnificat*[127] and in fine of the prayer which is chanted by the Card. Celebrant. While the anthem before the *Magnificat* is sung, the Pope puts incense into the thurible; the celebrant incenses the crucifix and the altar, and is incensed by the deacon, and the incensing continues as after the offertory at high-mass (See p. 21) At the *Gloria Patri* the deacon, having incensed the Card, priests, bows his head in the middle of the chapel, and then proceeds to incense the Card, deacons. After the prayer; *Ite Missa est, Alleluja, Alleluja*, is sung; and the choir answers, *Deo gratias Alleluja, Alleluja*: the Pope gives the usual blessing, the Celebrant publishes the indulgence of thirty years and this beautiful service terminates. In the sacristy His Holiness puts on a *mozzetta* of white (instead of red) damask, and wears it during the whole of Easter week: His shoes also are white. The Cardinals put on red *mantellette* and *mozzette* over their purple cassocks; these they afterwards change for others of scarlet.

Mass of Pope Marcellus.

The mass sung on this day is that of Pierluigi da Palestrina, called the mass of Pope Marcellus; not because it was composed during his pontificate; but because, according to Baini, Pierluigi had intended to dedicate a work to that Pope, to whom he was grateful and attached, but was disappointed by His Holiness' premature death; and therefore he persuaded Card. Vitellozzi to give it that name in honour of his former patron. This is the celebrated mass, which rescued ecclesiastical music from the dangers which surrounded it in the Pontificate of Pius IV (as we have related in The Papal Chapel, Rome, 1839), and not of Marcellus II, as Baini has proved. It is said, that when it was first sung in the papal chapel, the Card. dean Francesco Pisani was so enraptured with it, that he exclaimed with Dante, Paradise, Canto X.

Render è questo voce à voce in tempra

Ed in dolcezza, ch'esser non può nota

Se non colà dove il gioir s'insempra.

to whom, with all the readiness of the bucolic shepherds, whom this classic soil even now produces, Card. Sorbelloni, the Pope's cousin, replied:

Risponda dunque; O beata sorte!

Risponda alla divina cantilena

Da tutte parti la beata Corte,

Si ch' ogni vista ne sia pià serena.

Baini Mem. Stor. T. 1.

|*Ceremonies at S. John Lateran's.*

The ceremonies of holy-week are performed at S. John Lateran's[128] by the chapter of that protobasilica, and resemble for the most part those which we have already described. On holy-saturday however, in addition to the rites before mentioned, the font of the baptistery is blessed by the Card. Vicar, baptism is solemnly administered there to adults, the newly-baptised are confirmed in the church, ordination is conferred during mass upon candidates, for the priesthood. We shall treat briefly of these various ceremonies.

|*Blessing of the fonti: baptistery.*

After the twelve prophecies have been recited, the Card. Vicar, (as the representative of the Bishop of Rome) wearing a purple cope and a mitre, goes in procession from the tribune of the basilica to the baptistery[129]. He is preceded by acolythes bearing the paschal candle[130], and the cross and usual lights, as well as by the candidates for baptism and orders, and the chapter of the basilica. In the mean time the beautiful tract, As the stag thirsts for the fountains of water, etc. is sung[131]. His Em. then chants the prayers appointed for the benediction of the font; he divides the water with his hand in the form of a cross, exorcises it, touches it, signs it three times with the sign of our redemption, and pours some of it towards the four parts of the world, in allusion to the command of Christ: "*Go teach all nations, baptising them*" (Matt. XXVIII). He then dips the paschal candle three times into the water, singing, and each time raising his voice to a higher pitch than before: "May the power of the Holy Ghost descend upon the fulness of this font"; as when He descended, says Gavant, "in the form of a dove at the baptism of Christ represented by this candle plunged into the water". Then breathing three times on the water nearly in the form of a cross "that he may unite the Trinity with the cross" (as the same author observes) he continues the chant, and raises the candle from the water, alluding in the prayer to "the effect of baptism, which confers grace, *raising* the soul from sin to glory". (Gavant). The blessed water is then sprinkled upon the people, and some of it is reserved to be sprinkled in houses, etc. In order to sanctify the water still more, the Cardinal now pours into it, in the form of a cross, oil of catechumens and chrism; and mixes them with the water of the font, in the name of the Father, Son, and Holy Ghost. This last ceremony is intended to signify, according to mystical interpreters, such as Amalarius, Honorius, Durandus, etc. "the union of Christ by baptism with the members of the church" (Gavant). The prayers of this benediction, most of which are sung in the tone of the *preface* at ferial mass, contain beautiful allusions to the mention of water in the Old and New Testaments, as for instance: "O God, whose Spirit at the very beginning of the world was borne upon the waters, that the nature of water might even then conceive the power of sanctification; O God, who washing with waters the crimes of a guilty world, didst sign the figure of regeneration in the very out-pouring of the deluge; may this font receive of the Holy Ghost the grace of thy only begotten Son"[132].

|Baptism of adults.

The Cæremoniale Episcoporum prescribes that infants, except in danger of death, should not be baptised during the eight preceding days, that they may be reserved for holy-Saturday. The beginning of the baptismal service and the exorcisms are performed privately in the sacristy by the parish-priest, while the prophecies are read in church[133]. After the font has been blessed, the catechumens wearing a long white dress, and accompanied by their respective godfathers and godmothers, approach the font, and in turn ascend. In answer to the questions of the Cardinal (who is now vested in a white, and not a purple, cope,) having renounced Satan and all his works and pomps, they profess their belief in the articles of Christian faith, and their desire of baptism[134]: then assisted by their sponsors they are baptised by infusion in the name of the Father, Son, and Holy Ghost; they are anointed with chrism, receive a white garment, with a charge to bear it unspotted before the tribunal of Christ, and in fine a lighted taper, that "when the Lord shall come to the nuptials, they may meet him in the heavenly court unto life everlasting".

|Litanies and confirmation.

The litanies are sung, while the procession returns to the church, where the newly-baptised are confirmed in a side-chapel, and exhorted to perseverance in virtue, by the Cardinal[135]; the litanies are then continued, but cease while all kneeling venerate the heads of SS. Peter and Paul shewn from above the high altar; the procession afterwards returns to the tribune, where the mass of the day is sung, and orders are conferred by the Cardinal-Vicar.

Mass and ordination.

The orders of priests and deacons are often mentioned in the N. Testament: and the church, as S. Thomas observes, instituted the inferior orders. Subdeacons are mentioned by Pope Cornelius and S. Cyprian in the 3rd century, as well as acolythes, exorcists, and lectors. S. Augustine and S. Gregory Nazianzen speak of *ostiarii*; and the clerical tonsure is mentioned by S. Isidore at the beginning of the 5th century, as a rite established before his time. Orders are conferred by the laying on of hands and prayer, as the scripture teaches, and also by the delivery of the instruments belonging to each order: appropriate exhortations addressed to the candidates for the different orders are interspersed with the prayers prescribed in the pontifical. (On their antiquity the reader may consult Morinus de Ordinationibus, Martene de Antiquis Eccl. Ritibus, T. 2. etc.) The tonsure is given after the *Kyrie eleison* of the mass, the 4 minor orders after the *Gloria in excelsis*; subdeacons are ordained before the epistle, which one of them repeats; deacons after the epistle and finally priests after the first part of the tract. These last, after the imposition of hands, receive their peculiar vestments, viz. the stole hanging down in front, and the chasuble: their hands are anointed with oil of catechumens, and they receive a chalice containing wine and water, a paten with a host, and power to say mass. (Luke XXII, 19). After offerings of candle have been made to the ordaining Bishop, the new priests join him in saying mass[136]: and after the newly-ordained and baptised have communicated, the priests profess their faith by reciting the apostles' creed; they receive power to forgive and retain sins (John XX, 22, 23), they promise reverence and obedience to their ecclesiastical superior, and receive the bishops blessing, who then directs that masses and prayers be said by those whom he has ordained, and recommends himself to their prayers. In other respects the mass is similar to that of the Papal chapel[137]. Morcelli in his calendar in summing up the ceremonies of this day, having mentioned the station at S. John Lateran's, the baptism of Jews and Turks, and mass in the papal chapel, says that at the *Gloria, tonitrus tormentorum ab Arce fiunt, Æra templorum ac Turium sonant.*

Armenian Catholics:

Having spoken of the ceremonies of the Vatican and S. John Lateran's, we might consider our task as completed[138]. Yet one more *funzione* attracts our countrymen on this day; and we are therefore unwilling to bid them farewell, before it is ended. Come then to S. Biagio or to S. Gregorio Illuminatore, to assist at the Armenian mass; and on the road we may talk of the venerable and amiable Fathers who perform that solemn service, and of the nature of their liturgy.

SS. Bartholomew and Thaddaeus were the first apostles of Armenia: but it was not till the beginning of the 4th century, that the whole country became Christian in consequence of the divine blessing, which attended the zealous exertions of S. Gregory surnamed the Illuminator. In the 6th century great numbers of the Armenians were infected with the heresy of Eutyches, who denied that there were two natures in Christ: and to this error they afterwards added some others. In the pontificate of John XXII, about the year 328, a zealous Dominican bishop, called Bartholomew of Bologna, went as a missionary among them; and many of the Eutychians or Monophysites returned to the bosom of the Catholic church. In the 16th century the Catholics were so furiously persecuted by Zachary, a schismatical patriarch, that they fled and took refuge in other countries. They have at present two establishments at Rome, one of the Antonian monks at the church of S. Gregory Illuminator, behind the colonnade of S. Peter's; and a national *ospizio* at S. Biagio in strada Giulia.

their liturgy.

"The Armenians," says Palmer "have only one liturgy, which is written in the ancient Armenian language, and has been used by them from time immemorial. The whole groundwork and order of the Armenian liturgy coincides with the Cæsarean, as used in the time of Basil. This liturgy has, like most others, received many additions in the course of ages. There are several prayers extracted from the liturgy of Chrysostom, and actually ascribed to him" Vol. 1, Liturgy of Armenia. "The liturgy of Basil can be traced with tolerable certainty to the 4th century. Striking as are some of the features, in which it differs from that of Antioch, it is nevertheless evidently a superstructure raised on that basis: the composition of both is the same, i.e. the parts, which they have in common, follow in the same order. The same may be said of the Constantinopolitan liturgy, commonly attributed to S. Chrysostom, of that of the Armenian church, and of the florid and verbose composition in use among the Nestorians of Mesopotamia. So that the liturgy of Antioch, commonly attributed to S. James, appears to be the basis of all the oriental liturgies". Tracts for the Times, N. 63. The author then proceeds to state the grounds of the belief that the liturgies of Antioch, Alexandria, Rome and Gaul were of Apostolic origin; concluding thus "It may perhaps be said without exaggeration, that next to the holy scriptures they possess the greatest claims on our veneration and study". Padre Avedichian observes in his preface to the Armenian liturgy, that it was probably compiled by John *Mandagunense*, an Armenian patriarch of the fifth century.

Armenian high-mass.

We shall now give a brief account of their high mass, which we do the more readily, because Mr. Palmer represents it in a very mutilated form. The celebrant, whether priest or bishop, is vested in the sacristy: the vestments bear some resemblance to those of the Greeks. The beginning of the mass is the only part probably taken from the Roman liturgy, but it contains an invocation of the B. Virgin and of the saint of the day. When the celebrant goes up to the altar, the veil is drawn: he uncovers the chalice, blesses the host, which is like ours of unleavened bread; pours wine and water into the chalice, and recites the beautiful prayer of S. John Chrysostom: "O Lord our God, who hast sent our Lord Jesus Christ the celestial bread, the nourishment of the whole world; do thou bless this proposition etc." The veil is then drawn back, and the offerings, the altar, and the people are incensed. The Celebrant recites the prayer of the festival, followed by other prayers composed by S. John Chrysostom: the Trisagion is sung, and the gospel is carried in procession, and is kissed by one of the congregation. Then follow the epistle, gospel, and creed. After two prayers, and two benedictions imparted to the people; the offerings are carried in procession to the altar, the celebrant offers them up to God, and prays that Jesus Christ will make him worthy to consecrate, and receive his "holy and immaculate body and precious blood; for thou, O Christ our God, art he who offers and is offered". After he has washed his hands, he says "O Lord God of armies, let this victim become "the true body and blood of thy only begotten Son". He then blesses the people, says prayers which correspond to our preface and *Sanctus*, and pronounces the words of consecration. After he has said other prayers, and made the sign of the cross several times over the host and chalice, he invokes the holy Ghost, begging also that the body and blood of Christ may produce "the salvation of our souls and the remission of our sins". He then prays, through the merits of the holy sacrifice, for the whole world, the church and state, all conditions of men and for all the faithful departed: he invokes the intercession of the B. Virgin and all the Saints: he prays for the Pope and all present; and after other similar supplications, he says the *Pater noster*. The elevation takes place at this part of the mass, and also the blessing of the people with the consecrated host and chalice, accompanied by appropriate prayers. After the curtains have been drawn, the priest breaks the host, and puts a particle of it into the chalice: he then receives communion, blesses the people with the chalice and particle, and distributes communion; before its distribution the curtains are drawn back. When the ablutions and prayers after the celebrant's communion are ended, turning towards the people, he recites a prayer of S. John Chrisostom, which is followed by the last gospel. Then invoking the holy cross he blesses the people, who unite in praising God. He finally blesses them again, and distributes blessed bread (not consecrated) among them. At S. Gregorio Illuminatore Vespers are added and said *in circolo*: the clergy carry tapers; and the gospel is held up by the Celebrant to implore blessings on the people.

Reflections.

These ceremonies may appear singular to us, who are of a different clime and different customs; their music in particular is little in accordance with our taste, or notions of melody and harmony. Yet the remark of Montfaucon (Diario Italico) "æra Dodonæa dixisses", alluding to the brass kettles of the oracle (Potter Arch. Graec. B. 2, § 8) is an exaggeration. Their *flabelli* are of metal, of a round form, surrounded with little bells, which are sounded at the seraphic hymn, to express, if we might believe Cancellieri, "by the trembling of the hands, that of the blessed spirits, who assist at the throne of the Divine Majesty with fear and trembling". (Tre Pontific. Not. VI). Their mass is anticipated, but not at so early an hour as that of the Latin. (Even in the Latin church, permissions to say mass in the afternoon of this day have been granted by some Popes; they may be seen in Cancellieri. *Funz. d. Sett. S. p.* 183, 184). Amid the numerous differences between their rite and our own, the attentive spectator will not fail to remark the similarity of the substance and order of their liturgy, and of that of the Roman church; although, with the solitary exception of the beginning of the mass, both have existed independently of one another during the last 1400 years. This is a powerful argument in favour of the great antiquity, nay of the apostolic origin of their most important ceremonies, which may be traced through different channels to the *primitive* liturgies of Rome and Antioch. It is also one of those striking illustrations, which Rome presents, of the unity and catholicity of the church; and at the same time of the adaptation of her immutable doctrines and sacred practices to the feelings and customs of widely-separated nations who, having little in common but human nature, yet all acknowledge "one Lord, one faith, and one baptism". (Ephes. IV. 5); and all belong to "one fold and one shepherd". John X, 16.

Conclusion.

Having now considered in detail the various ceremonies of Holy Week at Rome, a philosophic mind will take a general review of them: and this question will very naturally suggest itself: What judgment ought I to form concerning them? am I to consider them as mummery, or superstition, or idolatry, as many most confidently pronounce, who are unacquainted with their nature, their origin, and their meaning; and at the same time are little accustomed from early infancy to any language or gesticulations save those of the tongue? or am I not rather to regard them as a solemn, and sacred, and pathetic, and most ancient expression of Christian faith and Christian feeling; which, united as it is with the noblest productions of divine inspiration and of Christian art may haply not only instruct and elevate the mind, but also enkindle in the soul flames of that pure and practical devotion, which this holy season demands from every follower of Christ? Let the reader decide for himself; but for our part, we envy not the mind or heart of him, who can prefer the former of these views. We shall ever bless God, that we have learnt in another school not to condemn the customs and manners of other countries and other people, merely because they differ from our own; and that we are disposed to attribute to signs the meaning attached to them by those who adopt them, and not that of our own fancies. Men of warmer climates than our own convey to others their sentiments and feelings by action as easily as by the tongue. Italians, as well as Greeks and Orientals, have inherited from their fathers a language of gesture more powerful and expressive than that of words. The Hebrew prophets, Isaiah, Ezechiel, and others, nay Christ himself, spoke by action as well by the tongue. God appointed in the old law innumerable ceremonies: Christ in the new law of spirit and truth instituted sacred rites, or sanctified those which previously existed: the early church imitated His blessed example: and they have been faithfully preserved as a precious inheritance till the present time. The very objection, that some of them were borrowed from Jews or Pagans, is a proof of their primitive antiquity: Christ or the church removed from them all profaneness or superstition, and then adopted and sanctified them. (See Wiseman's Letters to Poynder). If all parties unite in approbation of the illumination of the cupola of S. Peter's, and of the fireworks of S. Angelo, considered as outward demonstrations of the exultation of the church at the resurrection of her Divine Spouse; we shall ever admire also the expressions of christian feeling exhibited in the interior of her temples, whether they consist in ceremonies or words; and on this day emulating the transports of joy of the fervent and eloquent pilgrim to Jerusalem and Mount Sinai, when shall unite our voices with those of the angelic spirits in singing, *Alleluja*; "because Jesus Christ, our Lord, who was delivered up for our sins, rose again for our justification". Rome. IV, 24, 25.[139]

Footnote 111: (return)

Anciently in some churches, as Thomassin has shewn (de dierum Festorum celebratione lib. 2. c. 14), fire used to be struck from a flint to light the church-lamps etc. every day and particularly on Saturday, and the new fire was blessed; on holy Saturday however this ceremony was performed with great solemnity; and in the 11th century it was restricted to that day alone. At Rome in holy week this practice was not originally confined to holy Saturday, but was observed on the three days before easter: for the first *Ordo Romanus* directs, that on holy *thursday* fire should be struck from a flint outside the church, and blessed. Amalarius also (4e Ordine Antiph.) testifies that on good *friday* "new fire was enkindled and reserved till the nocturnal office". Leo IV however (A.D. 847) appears to have first ordered that on Easter Eve "the old fire should be put out, and new fire blessed and distributed among the people" (Homil. de cura Pastorali). For Pope Zachary, about the year 731. in answer to the enquiries of Boniface, bishop of Mayence, states that "on holy thursday, when the sacred chrism is consecrated, three lamps of a large size filled with oil collected from the different lamps of the church, and placed in a secret part of the said church, should burn there constantly, so that the oil may suffice till the third day, that is saturday. Then let the fire of the lamps which is used for the sacred font be renewed. But concerning the fire taken *ex cristallis*, as you have asserted, we have no tradition". Pouget (Inst. Cathol. l. 1) observes that the new fire is blessed with great solemnity on this day, "because the fire struck from a flint appears to be a type of Christ arising from the dead". Formerly not only the lights of the church, but all the fires of the city were enkindled from the blessed fire (as we learn from a MS. Sancti Victoris (ap. Martene, De ant. Eccl. Ritibus lib. IV, c. XXIV). "After the *Ite Missa est*" says the Ordinarium of Luke archbishop of Cosenza "the bishop gives his blessing, and immediately the deacon commands the people, saying "Receive the new fire from the holy candle, and having put out the old, light it in your houses in the name of Christ; then rejoicing they depart with the light". This custom is mentioned also in Leo IVth's homily above quoted.

Footnote 112: (return)

As for the Paschal candle, Anastasius says that Zosimus, who was elected pope in 417, gave leave that candles should be blessed in the churches. Bened. XIV, Merati and Gretser understand by these words, that that Pontiff only extended to the parish churches a custom already practised in the greater churches: however this may be, the blessing of this candle is at least as old as the time of Pope Zosimus. It is inserted in the ancient sacramentary of Pope Gelasius (A.D. 495). S. Augustine (lib. 15 de Civ. Dei) mentions some verses written by himself in praise of the paschal candle. S. Jerome also speaks of it in his epistles; and Ennodius bishop of Pavia in 519 wrote two formulas, according to which it might be blessed. Cancellieri, at the end of his *Funzioni della Settimana Santa*, describes two blessings of the paschal candle contained in manuscripts of the 12th century. Du Vert as usual rejects every mystical meaning of the candle: but why then should it be lighted on this night, and not on christmas and other nights? The 4th Council of Toledo, held in 633, states that the paschal candle is blessed, in order that we may receive the mystery of Christ's resurrection; and hence the abbot Rupert says, that the candle when lighted represents Christ's resurrection from the dead. That such is its meaning appears from the five holes made in it in the form of a cross, to represent the five wounds of Christ: in them the five grains of incense are fixed by the Deacon, in order to represent, according to Rupert, the spices applied to Christ's body by Joseph of Arimathea. In confirmation of this explanation, we may observe that this candle is not removed from the church till the gospel has been sung on Ascension-day when Christ departed from among men: and it is lighted at solemn mass before the *gospel* and at vespers before the *Magnificat* on the Sundays and holidays which occur between holy saturday and the ascension. To the same symbolical meaning of this candle we must attribute the ancient custom of affixing to it (as a symbol of Christ) a tablet on which the current year of our Lord and its indiction were marked: sometimes these, if not other chronological dates, were inscribed on the candle itself by the deacon, before he sang the *Exultet*, as Ven. Bede testifies, The same idea was preserved in the practice of forming the *Agnus Dei* with the wax of the paschal candle. "On this day" (holy saturday) says Durandus "the acolythes of the Roman church make *lambs* of newly blessed wax, or of the *wax of the paschal candle* of the preceding year mixed with chrism: on

Saturday in Albis they are distributed by the Lord Pope to the people in the churches". Amalarius likewise mentions this custom. It appears also from the two benedictions of Ennodius mentioned above, that the faithful used particles of the pascal candle as a preservative against storms: the good effects hoped for in this and similar cases are attributed to the prayers of the church, which God in His goodness has promised to hear. The paschal candle is painted according to an ancient custom.

"Ast alii *pictis* accendant lumina *ceris*".

S. Paulinus Nat. VI. S Felicis

Pierin del Vaga, whom Vasari considered as the most distinguished of Raffaello's assistants, was originally nothing more than a candlepainter. His creation of Eve at S. Marcello at Rome, and his frescoes in the Doria place at Genoa, are well-known; at the Vatican he assisted Giovanni d'Udine in his arabesques, Polidoro in his antique chiaroscuri, and executed some of the most beautiful historical paintings of the loggie di Raffaello. Hence may we judge of the versatility of his talents.

Footnote 113: (return)

Why does a deacon perform this ceremony? since other benedictions are reserved to bishops and priests. Rupert assigns as a reason, that Christ's body was wrapped in spices by his disciples, and not by the apostles whose successors are bishops and priests: besides, the hymn sung by the deacon is the præconium Paschale, or announcement of the Resurrection, which was first made by inferiors to their superiors, by the women to the apostles. We may add that both the fire and the 5 grains of incense are previously blessed by the priest, and in the præconium itself there is not any form of blessing, strictly speaking. In the church of Ravenna however the bishop used to bless this candle (S. Gregory ep. 28, lib. 9). In the Roman church, according to cardinal Gaetani, the last of the Cardinal priests usually blessed the fire, and the last Card. deacon lighted the *lumen Christi*, or triple candle, and the Paschal candle. The deacon used to bless the latter either at the steps of the presbytery, or from the ambo; and hence we find a marble column, intended to support it, fixed to the ambo in S. Clement's S. Laurence's, and S. Pancras' churches at Rome. See another marble column destined for the same use ap. Ciampini, Vet. mon. cap. 2.

Footnote 114: (return)

Martene (De antiquis Eccl. rit. lib. 4, c. 24) maintains that this hymn was composed by S. Augustine, and this opinion is adopted also by Baillet and Benedict XIV, and confirmed by a MS. pontifical of the church of Pavia of the 9th century, and other documents cited by Martene, ibid: it was corrected by S. Jerome, if we may believe an ancient Pontifical of Poitiers (quoted ibid.) The *chant* of this beautiful hymn is very ancient. "I have seen," says Baini "in many manuscripts both anterior and posterior to the 11th century the melodies of the preface, of the *Pater noster*, of the *Exultet*, and of the *Gloria* precisely such as the modern" (T. 2, p. 92). In a splendid roll of the Minerva (signed D. 1. 2) of the 9th century, are contained the *Exultet*, the solemn benediction of the baptismal font, and the administration of all the ecclesiastical orders. Nor is this the only roll containing the chant precisely similar to the modern. D'Agincourt left another to the Vatican library. See also MS. no. 333 of the Barberini library, of the year 1503.

Footnote 115: (return)

Prudentius speaks of the "guttas olentes" or odoriferous drops of the candle, and S. Paulinus of Nola of "odora lumina": hence P. Arevalo conjectures that the grains of incense were fixed in the paschal candle even at the time of Prudentius in the 4th century.

Footnote 116: (return)

In churches, at the words *Apis mater eduxit*, the lamps also are lighted. With regard to the triple candle, we may observe that on an ancient marble column preserved in the Piazza before the cathedral of Capua is a bas-relief representing the lighting of the paschal candle by means of a reed surmounted by 3 small candles, as the Canonico Natali testifies in a letter printed at Naples in 1776. The triple candle is mentioned in the Ordo Romanus of Card. Gaetano, in that of Amelius, and in a MS. Pontifical of the church of Apamea, ap. Martene. As Thomassin observes, "we light a candle divided into three in honour of the Trinity, considering that enlightened by Christ we know that recondite mystery". Gavant also gives the same explanation. In the Greek service the bishop gives his blessing, as often as he sings mass, with a triple candle. In the Latin church it is used only on holy Saturday.

Footnote 117: (return)

See Appendix.

Footnote 118: (return)

This custom is proved from the letter of Siricius Pope in the 4th century to Himmerius, from letters of S. Leo and Pope Gelasius, as well as other ancient documents (ap. Bened. XIV, Institut. prima ed lat.); and vestiges of it are preserved in the liturgy of the weeks of Easter and Pentecost. Ordinations were generally conferred before Christmas, as is evident from the lives of the early Popes. Baptism was administered before the great festivals of Easter and Pentecost, that the newly-baptised might be prepared to celebrate them worthily, and receive the graces therein commemorated. Perhaps another reason for selecting the eve of Easter may be found in the parallel drawn by S. Paul between baptism and Christ's death and resurrection (Rom. VI, 5 and foll.): "we who are baptised in Christ Jesus are baptised in his death. For we are buried together with him by baptism unto death: that as Christ is risen from the dead by the glory of the Father, so we also may walk in newness of life" etc.

Footnote 119: (return)

See on such subjects Del Signore's Institut. Hist. Eccles. with notes by Prof. Tizzani Cap. V. § 19 seq.

Footnote 120: (return)

See Comm. ad Ord. Rom. Mabillonii tom. 2, Mus. Ital. p. 95.

Footnote 121: (return)

According to the Ordo Romanus, children after baptism on this day were to take no food or milk before Communion "and on all days of Easter-week let them go to Mass, and let their parents offer for them, and let all communicate". As Cabassutius proves in his notitia Ecclesiastica sæculi primi, they used to receive the B. Sacrament under the form of wine alone. The bishop dipped his finger into the sacred blood, and then put it into the mouth of the child a practice observed in modern times in some parts of the East, according to the learned Maronite Abraham Ecchellensis; afterwards a little milk and honey was put into their mouths, as an emblem (according to John the deacon) of the promised land, to which they were called. This custom of giving communion to children was not of necessity for salvation, as Cardinal Noris proves in Vindiciis Augustinianis § 4, and the Council of Trent observes. In some places an abuse crept in of putting the milk and honey into the consecrated chalice, but it was prohibited by an African Council.

Footnote 122: (return)

In the 4th century, S. Basil writing to the clergy of Neocesarea observes, that the litanies, which they then used, were introduced after the time of S. Gregory Thaumaturgus (Epist. 63). In Gaul about the year 452, S. Mamertus bishop of Vienne appointed solemn litanies to be recited on the three *rogation* days. "At Rome," say Palmer, "no doubt litanies were in use at an early period, since we find that in the time of Gregory the great (A.D. 590), the appellation of litany had been so long given to processional supplications, that it was then familiarly applied to those persons who formed the procession". Vol. 1, p. 271. That holy Pontiff gave the following directions; "Let the litany of the clergy set out from the church of S. John the Baptist, the litany of the men from the church of the holy martyr Marcellus, the litany of the monks from the church of SS John and Paul: the litany of the handmaids of God from the church of the blessed martyrs Cosmas and Damian, the litany of the married women from the church of the blessed protomartyr Stephen; the litany of the widows from the church of the blessed martyr Vitalis, the litany of the poor and children from the church of the blessed martyr Cecilia". Vita S. Gregorii a Joanne Diacono, lib. 1, c. 42. That the litanies were recited on holy-saturday appears from several ancient *rites* quoted by Marlene (De Ant. Eccl. Ritibus, lib. 4, c. XXV, and lib. 1, c. I, art. 18). Palmer, wishing to defend the liturgy of the church of England, maintains the antiquity of litanies, but pretends that the invocations of saints were not originally contained in them, but were added to them in the west about the eighth century (vol. I, p. 289). From a passage in Walafridus Strabo he is led to admit that at *his* time (the ninth century) "these invocations must have been *for some time* in use, and accordingly manuscript litanies containing invocations have been discovered by learned men, which appear from internal evidence to be as old as the eighth century". He attempts however by *negative* arguments to shew, that these invocations are not more ancient than that period; although at the same time he confesses that "we have no *distinct account* of the *nature* of the service which was used on occasions of peculiar supplication during the earliest ages". p. 272. To his arguments we may oppose the *positive* testimony of Walafridus Strabo, who says "The litany of the holy names is believed to have come into use after Jerome, following Eusebius of Cesarea, had composed the martyrology". A long time, about three centuries, elapsed before the *canon* of the scriptures was determined; and it is not therefore surprising if the *canon* of saints, (if such it may be called), who died at considerable intervals, required some time for its formation. Invocations of the saints in ancient litanies may be seen ap. Martene (lib. 4f c. 27 and lib. 1, c. 1, art. 18). One would conceive from Palmer's account of the Ambrosian litany that it did not contain invocations of the saints, p. 276; yet in the Ambrosian processional, to which he alludes, we read as follows "Afterwards they go to the altar, were the litanies are recited on bended knees, in reciting which the *names of the saints* without *Intercede pro nobis* are sung aloud by the provost and clergy of the first collegiate church; and by the other clergy with *Intercede pro nobis* and this rite of singing the *litanies* and antiphons is observed in every other stational church". ap. Martene lib. 4, c. 28. In the Ordo Romanus also De Benedictione Ecclesiæ these invocations are found. The question however concerning their antiquity *in the litanies* is of minor importance. Even Palmer admits, that "Catholic fathers in the 4th century invoked the saints" p. 292, though he gravely assures his readers, that "they were too well instructed in the Christian faith to believe positively that the saints heard our prayers". He mentions the learned work of Serrarius called "Litaneutici seu de Litaniis etc." as an instance of the writings, in which "innumerable passages have been cited from ancient writers to prove, that the invocation of saints is more ancient than the eighth century. But most of those passages do not refer to the invocation of saints, but to prayers made to God for the intercession of saints". Palmer, vol. I, p. 278. We consider that there is little difference in principle between these two things: we shall however, to satisfy him, quote only one passage from an ancient Oriental liturgy. "Mother of our Lord Jesus Christ, pray for me to the only begotten Son, who was born of thee, that he may forgive me my offences and sins, and may receive from my feeble and sinful hands this sacrifice, which in my weakness I offer on this altar, through thy intercession for me, O holy Mother". (From the ancient liturgy used by the Nestorians called the liturgy of the holy apostles. Renaudot, t. II. See bishop Poynter's Christianity, Note E: and ancient inscriptions in Rock's Hierurgia, p. 347 and foll.) Though we have the *innumerable ancient* passages above-mentioned in favour of the Catholic doctrine, yet shall we call Mr. Palmer's attention to the following passage of his own work. Speaking of secrecy, he says: "this primitive discipline is sufficient to account for the fact, that very few allusions to the liturgy or eucharistic service are found in the writings of the Fathers". I, p. 14. His fears of *heresy and blasphemy* arising from the invocation of Saints may be calmed by the simple perusal of the doctrine of the church taught by the Council of Trent, sess. 25. "The holy synod commands all bishops and other teachers—*diligently to instruct the faithful, teaching them* that the Saints reigning with Christ offer to God their prayers for men; that it is *good and useful* to invoke them with supplication, and to have recourse to their prayers, help, and assistance, in order to obtain benefits *from God through his Son Jesus Christ our Lord, who alone is our Redeemer and Saviour*". Accordingly we say in the litany "Lord, have mercy on us: holy Mary *pray for us*" etc.

Footnote 123: (return)

We shall say nothing of sculptured figures taken from the catacombs, such as the statues of the good shepherd and S. Hippolitus now in the Vatican, or the numerous bas reliefs on Christian sarcophagi (on which see Raoul-Rochette, Tableau des Catacombes, c. IV. Beschreibung der Stadt Rom. B. 2, in the description of the Christian Museum in the Vatican Library). On another class of Christian representations the reader may consult Buonarruoti's *Osservazioni sopra alcuni frammenti di vetro, ornati di figure*. We shall rather call the attention of the Christian antiquarian to the numerous frescoes painted in the chapels of the catacombs, and illustrated by Bosio, Bottari, d'Agincourt etc., the latter of whom attributes some of them to the second century on account of the similarity of their style to that of frescoes in the tomb of the Nasones, which is situated on the Flaminian way at a short distance from Rome; his opinion is confirmed by the fact that some of them have been broken through, with the view of preparing a place of burial for the bodies of martyrs slain in *subsequent persecutions*. A list of their subjects which are *generally* taken from the old and new Testaments may be seen in Raoul-Rochette (c. 3, p. 157 foll. ed. de Brusselles). Of these we may briefly notice in particular some of the representations of Christ, of the B. Virgin, of the apostles and martyrs. In them Christ sometimes appears as an infant on the lap of His holy mother, Who ever pure and modest is always veiled; and this lovely group is found not only on these paintings, but also on bas-reliefs and glass-vessels generally anterior to the 4th century, and consequently to the general council of Ephesus held in 431; although it is pretended that such figures were first designed after that period. (Instances are enumerated by Raoul-Rochette c. VI). Constantina, daughter of Constantine, whose tomb is still preserved at Rome, begged of Eusebius bishop of Cesarea a likeness of our Divine Saviour (Concil. Labbe. t. VII, 493 seq): we must have recourse to the catacombs for His most ancient portraits. See one resembling the ordinary type of His sacred head and taken from the cemetery of Calixtus, at the end of Raoul-Rochette's work. This type, repeated again and again on Christian monuments during the last sixteen hundred years or more, may suggest the hope that some traces of our Divine Saviour's features are still preserved among us, notwithstanding the diversity of His portraits, of which S. Augustine complained, De Triniti l. 8, c, 4 5. Raoul-Rochette's opinion, that this likeness and the portraits of the apostles were of Gnostic origin, is altogether unsupported, as the Belgian editors of his work justly observe. Christ is frequently represented also as seated amid His apostles, of whom SS. Peter and Paul were favourite subjects of the old artists: see Raoul-Rochette c. VI, where he mentions, after the older antiquaries, the ancient representations of S. Ciriaca, S Priscilla, SS. Stephen, Cyprian, Laurence, Agnes, and other martyrs. During Diocletian's persecution, the provincial council of Eliberis in Spain decreed, that there should be no paintings on the walls of churches: its 36th canon was evidently intended to save sacred pictures from the profanations perpetrated by the pagans. The faithful however, fertile in expedients to gratify their devotion, now began to use those portable representations of pious subjects called diptychs, because they generally consisted of two tablets which could at pleasure be *folded* together. They were formed of ivory or wood, and resembled the presents of that name formerly sent by the consuls on the day of their entrance into office: on these were usually inscribed the names and the portraits of the new magistrates. (Symmachus lib. 2, ep. 80, all 71). The sacred diptychs, of which many are preserved in the Vatican Library, were easily saved from the fury of the Iconoclasts. Their folding form without their portability is preserved in many of the ancient altar-pieces of Italian and other churches and from them the modern altar-pieces are derived: they did not however supersede the use of frescoes, or mosaics, as is evident from innumerable ancient and modern ecclesiastical monuments of this city. In the preceding chapter we laid before our readers the doctrine of the catholic church concerning respect paid to images, p. 80.

Footnote 124: (return)

"He is risen; he is not here. But *go, tell* his disciples and *Peter*, that he goeth before you into Galilee". Mark XV, 6 7.

Footnote 125: (return)

This Hebrew word, which frequently occurs in psalms of praise, CIV, 34, CV, 45, CVI, 1, etc. has been preserved, as well as *Amen*, and *Sabaoth*, in its original form in most liturgies. According to S. Gregory (Ep. 64, ind. 2). who appeals to S. Jerome's authority, it was introduced into the Roman liturgy in the time of Pope Damasus. S. Gregory forbade it to be sung at funerals, (as it had been at that of Fabiola: S. Jerome in Epitaphio Fabiolæ;) or during Lent.

Footnote 126: (return)

Gavant and others, following Walafridus Strabo and the abbot Berno, think that the Offertory and *Agnus Dei* are not said, in order to signify the silence of the holy women returning from the sepulchre (Mark XVI, 8). Others attribute some of these omissions to the circumstance, that there is no communion; on this day, and therefore neither offertory or postcommunion; anciently however communion was given on this occasion, as is evident from the Gelasian sacramentary (See Bened. XIV, De Festis c. VIII). The kiss of peace, as Grancolas observes, is not given, because formerly at the dawn of easter-sunday, soon after the mass of easter-eve, the faithful used to assemble in the church "and kissing one another with mutual charity to say, *Surrexit Dominus* "; (the Lord is risen) Ordo Rom. ab Hittorpio ed. p. 55. Merati says, that the *Agnus Dei* is omitted because it is of recent origin, having been first introduced into the liturgy by Pope Sergius A.D. 688 (lib. Pont.), whereas the Mass of the day is of greater antiquity.

Footnote 127: (return)

Cancellieri says that the music of this *Magnificat* was composed by Luca Marenzio. Among the compositions prior to Palestrina, and still sung in the papal chapel, Baini reckons the Magnificats of Carpentrasso and Morales, as well as the *Te Deum* and *Lumen ad revelutionem gentium* of Costanzo Festa.

Footnote 128: (return)

This basilic, which is the cathedral of the bishop of Rome, was first erected by Constantine, whose statue taken from his baths adorns the portico. It was in great part destroyed by fire in 1308; but it was restored by the munificence of the Popes and the piety of the faithful, emulated in these days, in which we deplore the burning of S. Paul's. In the gothic tabernacle over the high altar are preserved the heads of SS. Peter and Paul. The mosaics of the tribune were made by order of Nicholas IV (A.D. 1278-1292).

Footnote 129: (return)

This baptistery, as well as the basilica, is attributed to the time of Constantine; it was reduced to its present state by Urban VIII; On an ancient and interesting Christian sarcophagus taken from the Vatican cemetery is represented a basilica with its apsis, and near it a circular building evidently meant for the baptistery: this is covered with a cupola surmounted by the monogram of Christ; and over the gate are curtains drawn up on each side, See Raoul-Rochette-Tableau des Catacombs, p. 332. The font is an ancient urn of basalt the paintings above it, between the second order of columns, representing, the life of S. John Baptist, are by Carlo Maratta.

Footnote 130: (return)

In a missal of Pavia it is called a figure of the column which preceded the Israelites going out of Egypt.

Footnote 131: (return)

The stag was a favourite subject of the early Christian artists, who often represented it in their paintings, and afterwards on their mosaics. The text above quoted explains its signification.

Footnote 132: (return)

"In most of the old rituals we find that the font was hallowed with various ceremonies besides prayer. It was customary to make the sign of the cross, as we learn from the testimony of Chrysostom, Augustine, and Pseudo-Dionysius". Palmer vol. 2, p. 195. Martene observes that the rite of pouring chrism into the water is mentioned in all the ancient Gallican, Ambrosian, and Mozarabic liturgies. The blessing of baptismal water is reckoned by S. Basil, in the 4th century, among apostolical traditions. (De Spiritu. S. c. 27).

Footnote 133: (return)

"Some form of admission to the class of catechumens was used in all churches at an early period, and it seems most commonly to have consisted of imposition of hands with prayers for the person. To this in many places were added various rites, such as, signing the forehead of the candidate with the cross, the consecration and giving of salt, which was entitled the sacrament of catechumens, repeated exorcisms, or prayers and adjurations to cast out the power of Satan, anointing with oil, and other mystical and figurative rites. In the course of many ages, when the Christian church had overspread the face of the world, and infidelity had become in most places extinct, the form of admission to the class of catechumens was from a veneration for old customs in many places conjoined to the office of baptism, and administered at the same time with it to the candidates for that sacrament whether they were infants or not". Palmer, vol. 2, c. 5, sect. 1.

Footnote 134: (return)

"It has been customary in the Christian church from the most remote period, for the candidates for baptism to renounce the devil and all his works, before they were admitted to that sacrament. This renunciation was always followed by a profession of faith in Christ, as it is now in the English liturgy. The last interrogation and answer "Vis baptizari, Volo" have long been used in the west. (Martene de Antiq. Eccl. rit. tom. I, p. 180, 192). According to the ancient custom of the Roman church, represented in the Sacramentary of Gregory, the profession of faith occurs between the hallowing of the water and the administration of the sacrament. This custom has long been used in the Roman church; since the Sacramentary of Gelasius (A.D. 494) appointed the confession of faith to be made immediately before baptism, *though the renunciations were made some hours before.* In primitive times the sign of the cross was not only made on the forehead of the elect at the time of baptism, but was used very often in other ways: this act is probably not more recent than the apostolical age; and this sign was made in some part of almost every Christian office. The administration of baptism was succeeded by various rites in the primitive church; among other the newly-baptised were clothed in white garments. Formerly also confirmation followed immediately after baptism". I have extracted the preceding passages from different sections of Palmer's 5th chapter, vol. 2: coming from a clergyman of the church of England, they are important admissions, and they dispense with the necessity of my proving the antiquity of these various baptismal riles. The reader may see proofs of them collected in Palmer (loc. cit.) Martene T. 1: cap. 2, etc.

Footnote 135: (return)

Palmer says, that in confirmation, to the rites of prayer and imposition, of hands was added "that of anointing with an unguent or chrism, made of oil and balsam, and hallowed by the prayers of the bishop.—We learn from the writings of Tertullian and Origen, that it was already customary both in the east and the west at the end of the 2nd or beginning of the 3rd century. This chrism was intended to signify the grace of the Holy Spirit then conferred". Palmer, Or. Lit. vol. 2, p. 199. If this unction had not been of apostolic origin, it would not have been customary in all churches at so early a period.

Footnote 136: (return)

At S. John Lateran's, when the *Agnus Dei* is said, the ancient custom is preserved, which was originally established by Pope Sergius, of saying *Miserere nobis* three times, and not *Dona nobis pacem*, which words were introduced into the liturgy, (according to Innocent III, De Myst Missæ) about the 10th century, in time of schism.

Footnote 137: (return)

Orders are generally conferred on the saturday of each ember-week, besides the saturday before passion and easter sundays. A minute detail of the numerous ceremonies of ordination can not be expected in a work on the ceremonies of holy-week. The reader may find them all enumerated in the Pontifical, and on their antiquity he may consult Morinus, De Ordinationibus; Martene, De Ant. Eccl. Rit. t. 2. etc. On the service of holy saturday see the MS. Pontifical of the Apamean church and various Ordines ap. Martene, lib. IV, c. 24. Formerly after the mass there was general communion; and at Rome no Vespers were said (Alcuin), and 7 altars were consecrated.

Footnote 138: (return)

In the afternoon the parish-priests bless with prayers and holy water the houses and paschal food of their parishioners. In the Ordo Romanus, besides the blessing of milk and honey, there is a formula of benediction of a lamb and other food. Durandus also (lib. 6 Ration.) mentions the blessing of the lamb, a custom which is preserved at Rome till the present time. The shops of the *pizzicaroli* are illuminated and gaily decorated, probably because *they* have peculiar reasons to rejoice at the conclusion of the *austerities* of lent.

Footnote 139: (return)

For the ceremonies of Easter-sunday see The Pontifical Mass sung at S. Peter's on Easter-sunday etc. By C.M. Baggs. D.D. Rome 1840.

APPENDIX

PECULIAR CEREMONIES OF HOLY-WEEK AT JERUSALEM

Having spoken of the blessing of the paschal candle at Rome, we may for a few moments turn our thoughts towards a city still more ancient, and trodden by holier and more exalted beings than even the apostles and martyrs of the eternal city. The justly-celebrated traveller John Thevenot in his Voyage du Levant describes the ceremonies of holyweek performed at Jerusalem; the distribution of palms, the washing of the feet on Maunday-Thursday at the door of the holy Sepulchre; and the procession to the holy places or stations performed by the Catholic Christians. Concerning this the eloquent Pere Abbé de Geramb, in his interesting Pelerinage at Jerusalem in 1832, informs us that "by means of a figure in relief of the natural size, whose head, arms, and feet are flexible, the religious represent the crucifixion, the descent from the cross, and the burial of Jesus Christ, in such manner as to render all the principal circumstances apparent to the senses and striking".

Both these distinguished writers of different periods agree in testifying, that all the devotions of the Catholics were and are still conducted with so much order that they are admired both by Christians and Turks, whereas those of the schismatical Christians took place with much confusion, and with such a noise, that the Janissaries, who had to preserve order, were obliged to strike the persons engaged in them as well as the spectators. This statement is confirmed by the account, which they and other travellers give, of the *holy fire* of the Greeks and other schismatics. Benedict XIV observes that no mention is made of the supposed miracle of the holy fire by early Christian writers who lived at Jerusalem; as Eusebius, S. Jerome, S. Epiphanius, or S. Cyril bishop of Jerusalem. It is however spoken of by Bernard a Frank monk of the ninth century, and in a Pontifical of the church of Poictiers of about the tenth century: by Hugo Flaviniacensis in Chronico Virdunensi, in the discourse of Urban II in the council of Claremont, and in other documents of the middle ages mentioned by Martene (lib. IV, c. XXIV). Lupi (tom. 4, Conc. gen. etc.) thinks it probable, that the custom of burning lights and the paschal candle on this day was instituted, in order to return thanks to God for a miracle (which *may* of old have happened at Jerusalem) and to announce it to all nations.

I shall now extract a brief account of the scene of confusion enacted in modern times at Jerusalem on such occasions from Thevenot, in whose work is a print representing it. "After our Catholic office was ended" says he, "we prepared to enjoy the sight of the holy fire of the Greeks, Armenians and Copts, whose priests make their people believe, that on holy Saturday fire descends from heaven into the holy Sepulchre, and on that account make each of their pilgrims, who are very numerous, pay some money. This solemnity appears rather a comedy or a farce than a church-ceremony, and is very unbecoming in a place so sacred as the holy Sepulchre. After we had finished our service, which was about eight in the morning, they, extinguished all their lamps and those of the holy Sepulchre, and then they commenced their folly, running round the holy Sepulchre, like mad people, crying, howling, *et faisans un bruit de diables*; it was charming to see them running one after another, kicking and striking one another with cords; many of them together held men in their arms, and going round the holy Sepulchre, let them fall, and then raised horrible shouts of laughter, while they who had fallen ran after the others to avenge themselves: it seemed that both old and young were downright mad. From time to time they raised their eyes, and stretched their hands, full of taper, to heaven, crying all together *eleison*, as if they were wearied at the delay of the holy fire. This scene continued till towards three in the evening, when two Greek archbishops and two bishops habited as patriarchs, for the patriarch was not then at Jerusalem, left their choir with all their clergy, and began the procession round the holy Sepulchre: they were joined by the Armenians, four of whom wore mitres: then came a Coptic bishop, with all his clergy and people. After they had walked three times round the holy Sepulchre, a Greek priest came out of the chapel of the Angel, which is close to that of the holy Sepulchre, and gave notice to him who represented the Patriarch, that the holy fire had descended from heaven: the latter then entered into the holy Sepulchre, followed by the representatives of the Armenian patriarch and of the Coptic bishop. After they had remained there a short time, we saw the Greek archbishop in an amusing posture, bending down his head, and bearing in each hand a quantity of lighted tapers. No sooner had he appeared, than all rushed one upon another to light their tapers from those of the archbishop; as that is considered the best fire, which is first lighted. The Janissaries however, who were stationed near the door of the chapel of the Angel, did not stand with their arms folded, but made the calpacs and turbans of the Greeks fly from one end of the church to the other, striking around on all sides with their sticks, to make way for the poor archbishop, who also as we may suppose did all in his power to save himself. He then mounted in haste a stone-altar opposite the entrance of the holy Sepulchre, where he was immediately surrounded by the people: those also who had lighted their tapers endeavouring to save themselves were overwhelmed by the others: the confusion was horrible, and blows were not unfrequent. After the Greek archbishop has come out, the Armenian appears, and saves himself from the crowd in the church of the Armenians, and the Copt in that of the Copts. Every one was in such a hurry to get some of the holy fire, that in a moment more than 2000 bundles of candles flamed in the church: and the people, crying out like persons possessed began greater follies than before. A man carrying a drum on his back began to run with all his might round the holy Sepulchre, and another running in the same manner struck it with two sticks; and when he was tired, another immediately took his place. *"Il semble qu' on soit dans un enfer, et que ce soient tout autant de diables déchainès."*—But enough of this unedifying scene, of which the Abbé Geramb gives a similar account. If we contrast with it the majestic and edifying ceremonies of the Roman church, we shall feel grateful to God for having preserved us from such disorders. I shall merely add from Thevenot, that the Christians are called to office at the holy Sepulchre by boards struck with iron, as we are for two days in holy-week: but drums and other instruments are also played there, which make, he (adds), "une musique enragée".

The distinguished missionary and pilgrim D. Casto Gonzalez recounts other disorders of the Greeks during Holy Week, and profanations of the most holy sanctuaries of Palestine. In the year 1833 he exposed, but not without great risk, the fraud of the "holy fire". On the holy-Saturday of the Greeks the officiating Bishop accompanied by an Armenian and a Coptic Bishop and their respective clergy had already walked thrice round the holy Sepulchre, when the missionary ignited a match with phosphorus, and holding it up exclaimed "Look, the heavenly fire has fallen into my hands": he then extinguished it and lighted it again several times to the great astonishment of the assembled multitude. He was protected by the Turks from the dangers which surrounded him. So manifest was the fraud of the pretended "holy fire" that even the schismatical Armenian patriarch issued a circular letter forbidding his spiritual subjects to be present at the disgraceful exhibition.

The Pere Abbé de Geramb gives a glowing account of the Catholic service and mass on holy saturday; and we most warmly recommend to our readers the perusal of the 34th *Lettre* of his *Pelerinage*, in which he describes all the ceremonies of holy week at Jerusalem, where they are invested with the peculiar charm arising from spots so sacred, where Christ suffered, and died, and rose again. Though in other respects the Roman ceremonies are of a more exalted nature, yet here must we be contented to transport ourselves in imagination to those beloved sanctuaries, and to see the *representation* of the holy Sepulchre at S. Maria Egiziaca. We shall conclude with the words of the distinguished writer: "Jamais douleur n'affecta plus vivement mon àme, que celle qui s'en empara au moment où je m'arrachai pour jamais de l'église du saint Sepulcre. Taut que je vivrai elle sera aussi présente à mon esprit que profondément gravée dans mon coeur; toujours souvenir me fera tressaillir, parce que toujours, et plus qu' aucun autre souvenir, il me rappellera Jésus, crucifié pour mon salut, pour la salut du genre humain, à l'amour duquel nous devons repondre par le plus vif, le plus tendre, le plus absolu de tous les amours; ce Jésus auquel je dois l'ineffable bonheur de comprendre, de sentir cette grande verité, que je voudrais faire comprendre et sentir a l'univers entier, que lui seul est tout, que tout ce qui n'est pas lui, n'est rien, n'est que neant". Pelerinage à Jerusalem, Lett. 36.